CONTENTS

W9-CMH-120

PENNSYLVANIA

NORTHWESTERN

NORTH CENTRAL

NORTHEASTERN

CENTRAL

SOUTHWESTERN

SOUTH CENTRAL

SOUTHEASTERN

This is for Croy,
1928–1993.
He made his journey with humor, grace,
kindness, and dignity.

ACKNOWLEDGMENTS

This book is much better than it might have been because of suggestions and help from a number of old friends, Pennsylvanians all, who made sure I didn't miss good places. Instead of using the usual author's cryptic phrase, "They know who they are," I'll tell you who they are and say, "They know what they did." Thanks to: John Andrews, Peter Burnet, Tig Burnet, Sister Joan Chittister and the Benedictine sisters of Erie, Carole Coyne, Evan Homan, Sarah Homan, Don Hopey, Kerry Lacey, Jane Musala, Sister Maureen Tobin, Dick Trinca, Judy Trinca. I miss you.

OFF THE BEATEN PATH™ SERIES

Pennsylvania

OFF THE BEATEN PATH™

FOURTH EDITION

SARA PITZER

A Voyager Book

The Globe Pequot Press

Old Saybrook, Connecticut

ABOUT THE AUTHOR

Sara Pitzer is a freelance writer. Before she began writing books, she worked as a feature editor and writer for a Pennsylvania newspaper and wrote for magazines. She considers herself, above all, a reporter, and she prides herself on describing what she sees objectively and accurately.

In addition to *Pennsylvania: Off the Beaten Path,* Sara has written *North Carolina: Off the Beaten Path; Cat Tales; Recommended Country Inns: South,* and *Enjoying the Art of Southern Hospitality.*

Sara lives in the country with two dogs and half a dozen cats.

Pennsylvania Wineries listing reprinted from *Pennsylvania Wines and Wineries,* courtesy of The Pennsylvania Wine Association.

Off the Beaten Path is a trademark of The Globe Pequot Press

Cover map © DeLorme Mapping
Text illustrations by Carol Drong

Library of Congress Cataloging-in-Publication Data
Pitzer, Sara.
    Pennsylvania : off the beaten path / Sara Pitzer. — 4th ed.
        p.   cm.— (Off the beaten path series)
    "A voyager book."
    Includes index.
    ISBN 0-7627-0072-6
    1. Pennsylvania—Guidebooks.   I. Title.   II. Series.
F147.3.P57   1997
917.4804'43—dc21   96-52521
                                                                         CIP

Manufactured in the United States of America
Fourth Edition/Second Printing

INTRODUCTION

Pennsylvania schoolchildren used to belt out a song with these lyrics:

Pennsylvania forever
Wonderful keystone state
Beautiful, rugged, glorious
Fashioned sublime and great.

They understood it. Oh sure, the part about "fashioned sublime and great" translated into "fashion sub lime and grape," which everyone supposed had something to do with a stylish variation on lemonade, probably made up in the mountains somewhere. But the rest made sense: Pennsylvania was one of the thirteen original colonies, located among those colonies in the same position that an architectural keystone is in an arch—they learn that in the fifth grade unit on Pennsylvania, probably from Miss Young, who must've taught every fifth grader in the state. As for beautiful, rugged, and glorious, they saw it every day. Even in the meaner coal towns, mountains soared above the sooty sidewalks, glowing green under the sun in spring and summer, gilded with the colors of changing foliage in fall, and glinting with ice and snow in the winter. No matter where a Pennsylvania kid lived, it wasn't far to a hike in the woods or fishing in a stream or swimming in a pond. Waterfalls, rivers, and woods—these were things for a Pennsylvania kid to be proud of.

Other verses in the song praised the state's industries: lumber, iron, coal, oil, and steel. Everyone understood. That was the good, honest work parents did. It was something to be proud of, too. So was farming.

And, of course, the history was special. No other state had the Declaration of Independence or the Liberty Bell. No other state had Philadelphia, Birthplace of a Nation. A kid was pretty lucky to be a Pennsylvanian.

Those lessons stuck.

As the economics of Pennsylvania changed, mining deposits ran out or demand dwindled, and major industries staggered under foreign competition, times got tough. But the waterfalls, rivers, and mountains remained beautiful, rugged, glorious, fashioned sublime and great. The history remained special. The kids became adults and reared their own kids, still knowing where to find a good place to fish or swim or hike. Still proud. They helped make and keep Pennsylvania the great place to explore that it is today.

Tourism is the second most important industry in the state today. (Manufacturing still holds first place.) By and large, it's related to the state's important history and to its magnificent geographic attributes.

Determined Pennsylvanians worked fervently, especially around the time of the American Bicentennial, on historic preservation and restoration projects. The splashiest projects are the famous ones—Independence Hall in Philadelphia; Valley Forge National Historical Park, commemorating Washington's victory over the British; and the Gettysburg National Military Park, scene of a major Civil War battle, for instance. But the projects with heart are those where citizens in smaller communities studied up on what was special about their history and set about bringing it to life, generally investing their own money and time and lots of their own sweat. For example, the people of Mifflinburg knew that their town had once produced more buggies per capita than any other town in the country. They bought and restored one of the buggy factories and now maintain the museum and take visitors through demonstration tours, all with volunteer labor. Several years ago they were able to burn the mortgage. In Aaronsburg, volunteers built a reproduction of an outdoor brick oven for the women of the Bicentennial Committee to demonstrate colonial baking and cooking. Such projects are the stuff of this book.

Geographically, in spite of areas of highly commercial tourism, which have their place, mind-boggling areas of forestland, as well as miles and miles of river and lakeshore, remain unspoiled because Pennsylvanians have stayed proud enough to protect them. In the northern tier, mostly wilderness, you can drive for hours, imagining that you've seen enough empty space to isolate every small warring country in the world. The rest of your life wouldn't be enough time to explore it all. Pennsylvania has 110 state parks. Only a few are described here. For a complete list with addresses and telephone numbers, write the Bureau of Travel Development, Pennsylvania Department of Commerce, 416 Forum Building, Harrisburg 17120.

Other attractions change and grow. In recent years the Amish have moved from a few areas of concentration, such as Lancaster, to farm in nearly all the fertile rural areas of the state. Everyone is trying to avoid duplicating the tourist density and corresponding circus that developed around Lancaster. The Amish attractions included here are all in low-key settings where the Amish welcome your business but desperately want to maintain their privacy.

In the past twenty or so years, wineries have flourished all over Pennsylvania. Fewer than two decades ago, only a few produced enough wine to sell, and even home wine makers hesitated to say in more than whispers that they produced alcohol. Prohibition wasn't so long in the past. As Pennsylvania vineyards have matured, so have the skills of the wine makers and the attitudes of the neighbors. So have the wines! More than fifty wineries throughout the state invite visitors for tours and sales. Because many of them are tiny, it is imperative that you call or write before you visit, if only to be sure someone will be available to show you around and pour a few tastes when you arrive. The larger wineries are more geared for short-notice visitors. A few of them appear in the text. The rest are listed at the end of the book.

I learned about some of Pennsylvania's wilderness and natural areas from Marcia Bonta's excellent book, *Outbound Journeys in Pennsylvania,* published by Keystone Books. For longer descriptions of some natural areas and for a more complete list of them, you might order a copy, for $12.75, by writing The Pennsylvania State University Press, University Park 16802.

With all this to do, how are you going to fit it all in? You're not—not in one seven-day trip, not even in one thirty-day trip. These experiences need to be savored, not raced through on a tight schedule. Try working a few small areas at a time, going home, and then coming back.

Don't forget your map when you come. The Pennsylvania Department of Transportation map shows the mountains and forests clearly, as well as most of the parks and natural areas. It may be sent to you when you write for your list of state parks. If not, write the Bureau of Office Services, Pennsylvania Department of Transportation, Harrisburg, PA 17120. The map of New Jersey and Pennsylvania published by the American Automobile Association shows roads clearly and identifies some small places not included on the PennDOT map.

One warning about maps and driving in Pennsylvania: Never assume that the shortest distance between two points is what it seems to be on the map, especially in the mountainous parts of the state. You have to experience it to know how winding and hilly some of those short-looking routes can be. The map just can't show what's really there. But then, that's what traveling off the beaten path is all about, isn't it?

A personal note. Although I was born in the South and live there now, I grew up in Pennsylvania, married a Pennsylvanian, and raised my children there. I traveled the back roads when they were still the main roads, working and living all over the state. Most of what I remembered as good remains; the changes, by and large, are improvements. I guess Thomas Wolfe couldn't go home again, but for me it turned into a helluva good time. I know it will for you, too.

By the way, that song ends:

> *Where ever I roam*
> *I will always say*
> *That my home*
> *Is Penn—-syl—-van—-i—-aaaaaa!*

I'm proud.

The prices and rates listed in this guidebook were confirmed at press time. We recommend, however, that you call establishments before traveling to obtain current information.

Southwestern Pennsylvania

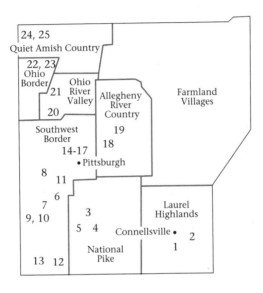

24, 25
Quiet Amish Country

22, 23
Ohio
Border

Ohio
River
Valley
21

Allegheny
River
Country

Farmland
Villages

20

Southwest
Border
14-17

19

18

• Pittsburgh

8

11

6

7

9, 10

3

5   4

Connellsville •

Laurel
Highlands

2

1

National
Pike

13   12

1. Fallingwater
2. Ohiopyle State Park
3. Scenery Hill
4. Always Christmas
5. Century Inn
6. Lemoyne House Historical Museum
7. Bradford House
8. Meadowcroft Village
9. Good Intent
10. Greene County Historical Museum
11. June Stout Antiques
12. Willow Inn
13. Log Cabin Bed and Breakfast

14. Carnegie
15. Pittsburgh Zoo
16. Carnegie Science Center
17. Cathedral of Learning
18. Trillium Trail
19. Beechwood Farms Nature Reserve
20. Old Economy Village
21. Richmond Little Red School
22. McConnells Mill State Park
23. Slippery Rock Gorge
24. Wendell August Forge
25. Candleford Inn Bed and Breakfast

SOUTHWESTERN PENNSYLVANIA

LAUREL HIGHLANDS

Everyone who visits Pennsylvania should see ◆ **Fallingwater,** the famous summer retreat that the architect Frank Lloyd Wright designed for the Pittsburgh department-store owner Edgar J. Kaufmann more than half a century ago.

The only remaining Wright house where the original setting, furnishings, and artwork remain intact, Fallingwater has attracted more than a million people since it opened to the public in 1964, which seems to take it out of the class of hidden-away places; remarkably, it retains a feeling of seclusion and oneness with the natural environment, especially if you go during the week or in the off-season to avoid peak crowds.

The house, surrounded by rhododendrons and seemingly growing out of the boulders and rocks, extends over a natural waterfall and the racing water of Bull Run. A gray sandstone four-story chimney at the core of the house anchors it into the stone cliff. Architects and laypeople alike know about the genius of Wright's designs, which allow the house to merge with its environment outside and to echo outdoor nature in its stone and wood interior. But touring Fallingwater, you see some of Wright's human idiosyncrasies reflected in the structure as well. For instance, tall men hunch under the low ceilings because Wright designed according to his own height—several inches under 6 feet. And a guide explains that the family asked Wright's permission before making even so simple an interior change as building bookshelves in a bedroom.

Looking about the place you can't help but wonder what it would've been like to live there. Cool in summer, certainly; but thinking of the chill that would get into the stone floors in the dead of winter, when ice and snow have settled into the landscape, stiffens your arthritis even as you're touring. Fallingwater was designed as a weekend "cottage," however, so in all likelihood no one spent much time there in zero-degree weather.

Fallingwater is maintained by the Western Pennsylvania Conservancy. At the end of your tour, they'll ask you to watch a short film about their organization's activities. Don't miss it.

Fallingwater

Unlikely as it sounds, the film is fascinating, and the work the conservancy does lifts your spirits. You may decide to join, even if you live out of state.

Children under age nine cannot tour Fallingwater, but that doesn't mean you have to skip the visit if you are traveling with small children. For $2 each you can leave them in a day-care center while you take the tour.

Fallingwater is about two hours southeast of Pittsburgh via the Turnpike, on Route 381, between the villages of Mill Run and

Ohiopyle. The house is open for tours from April through mid-November every day except Monday, 10:00 A.M. to 4:00 P.M. From December through March it is open only on weekends. A moderate admission fee is charged. Because the place has become so popular, you have to phone ahead for reservations. For more information, write P.O. Box R, Mill Run 15464 (412–329–8501).

After visiting Fallingwater, returning quickly to busy streets and stores feels inappropriate. Stopping for a walk or a picnic along the Youghiogheny River at ❖ **Ohiopyle State Park,** just 5 miles south on Route 381, eases you back into the modern world. The park covers almost 18,500 acres. Two state game lands next to it extend the wilderness farther. The **Youghiogheny Gorge,** cut 1,700 feet into the Laurel Ridge by the river, takes your breath away.

NATIONAL PIKE

From the park, traveling south on Route 381 takes you quickly back to Route 40, known as the National Pike. In colonial times it was the main road connecting Washington, D.C., with points west.

About 12 miles east of Washington, Pennsylvania, the National Pike runs straight into the little town of ❖ **Scenery Hill,** where you can browse through a number of antiques and specialty shops. ❖ **Always Christmas,** on the ground floor of an 1812 brick house that once housed runaway slaves, specializes in handmade Christmas tree ornaments and dolls. Call (412) 945–5177 for more information.

When you're through shopping, walk down the street to ❖ **Century Inn,** a twenty-one-room village inn that has been operating continuously since 1794. In the 1820s Andrew Jackson and Lafayette climbed from stagecoaches to sleep and eat here. Today lunch and dinner are served daily (only dinner on Sundays) from mid-March to mid-December. Breakfast is served only to those who stay in one of the inn's guest rooms. The cost of breakfast is included in the basic room rate figure, financially speaking. The cost to *your* figure is something else again. Breakfast includes waffles, bacon, scrambled eggs, juices, and homemade cinnamon rolls. Barry and Ellen Gardner, once publishers of the travel newsletter *Uncommon Lodgings,* who are fussy about their food and their beds, stayed here and loved it. Barry said that it "felt like a real country inn."

Part of the fun of visiting the inn is studying the antiques, including old kitchen tools clustered around the 7-foot fireplace. An impressive collection of antique toys and dolls fills one whole room upstairs.

Recreational facilities include tennis and volleyball courts and a hot tub. You'll be glad of a place to get some exercise if you have indulged in a meal at the inn.

The dining room serves homemade breads and a tasty assortment of near-trendy concoctions: peanut soup, Brie baked with butter and almonds, and coconut cream pie, for instance.

The inn is popular, so reservations are important whether you want to spend the night or dine or both. Write Century Inn, Scenery Hill 15360; phone (412) 945–5180.

SOUTHWEST BORDER

Once you arrive in downtown Washington, visit ◆ **LeMoyne House Historical Museum,** at 49 East Maiden Street, originally the home of antislavery advocate Francis LeMoyne and a shelter on the underground railroad. The house was built in 1812, and although its Civil War involvement made it historic, much that you see here is interesting because of what you learn about life *before* the Civil War. For instance, growing in a garden next to the house you'll find the herbs that Dr. LeMoyne kept when he lived here. The semiformal garden is divided to feature four categories of herbs: medicinal herbs for Dr. LeMoyne's medical practice, culinary herbs for his kitchen, and fragrant and flowering herbs for pleasure. Walking through the garden you can enjoy the low-growing sweet woodruff and the exotic flowering foxglove (from which digitalis to treat heart disease is extracted). The mints romp here and there, trying to defy their borders, and the astringent smell of southernwood reminds you of the cleaning and disinfecting that must have gone on in the house. Iris line the garden walks in spring, replaced through summer and autumn with zinnias and brown-eyed Susans.

Also inside the house, a nineteenth-century apothecary exhibit fills one room. Another interesting feature is the crematory, located in a separate building. You can tour the crematory on Sunday May through September from 2:00 to 4:00 P.M. It was the first one in the United States.

Other exhibits in the house, always related to the history of the area, change regularly. For example, one popular exhibit has been "Victorians at Home." A phone call will get you pertinent information about special exhibits during the time you plan to visit. Appropriately, the Washington County Historical Society operates from here, too. Tours run February through mid-December, Wednesday through Friday noon to 4:00 P.M., Sunday 2:00 to 4:00 P.M. Modest rates are charged. Call (412) 225–6740.

At 175 South Main Street, tour ◆ **Bradford House,** once the home of David Bradford, a leader in the Whiskey Rebellion of 1794. The home is furnished in antiques of the period and is open May 1 to December 20, Wednesday through Saturday 11:00 A.M. to 4:00 P.M., Sunday 1:00 to 4:00 P.M. Candlelight tours are held Friday to Sunday December 6, 7, and 8 from 6:00 to 9:00 P.M. The admission fees are modest. Call (412) 222–3604. As part of your visit, you may want to stop in the gift shop, which sells a number of items that appeal to kids. For instance, the William Trent Militia Company, which does reenactments of battles, also makes musket balls, dice, and lead pencils as the early soldiers made them. Books tell about the Whiskey Rebellion, about how children lived at the time, and what life was like for their parents.

Another great place to go with children is ◆ **Meadowcroft Village,** a bit under 20 miles northwest of Washington, 2½ miles west of Avella on Star Route 50. This historic site, developed by Albert and Delvin Miller, preserves the family's history of farming and breeding and racing horses. Some buildings have been brought in from other locations to re-create all the village activities. Tours include demonstrations of baking and blacksmithing and a chance to sit in an old one-room schoolhouse with a potbellied stove. Outside you can tour an antique train car that was a private dining car dating from the late 1800s. The Country Kitchen serves light meals, or you can use the outside picnic tables to eat a packed lunch. Meadowcroft Village is open Memorial Day through Labor Day Wednesday to Saturday from noon to 5:00 P.M. In May, September, and October it's open weekends only. Moderate rates are charged. Call (412) 587–3412.

If you're interested in strange little towns for their own sake, rather than for the attractions in them, travel west from Washington on Route 40, almost to the West Virginia border, to

◈ **Good Intent,** at the headwaters of Wheeling Creek's Robinson Fork. There's nothing here. Nobody knows how the village got its name, but it seems to be apt. And it seems to have started being apt almost from the beginning of the town's history. In the early 1800s Peter Wolf built a gristmill here. The mill pond filled up with silt, so he had to start over farther downstream. They never got around to creating a main street in town. Two gristmills, two blacksmiths' shops, a tannery, a stage company, a harness and saddle shop, a post office, and a Baptist church have all come—and gone. Nobody teaches in the schoolhouse. Somebody lives in it. The general store doesn't sell anything but coal and woodstoves, and it's only open on Saturday. There's more: The town doesn't have a local government, but it does have an unofficial mayor, who lives somewhere else.

Folks who live here like it just the way it is. They say that along with all the things Good Intent doesn't have, it also doesn't have crime, hurry, legal contracts, or selfishness. People help each other in times of sickness. They seal agreements with nothing more than a handshake. The reporter Don Hopey was so taken with the peace of this place that he wrote about it for the *Pittsburgh Press* and suggested including it in this book. He interviewed a local couple who liked the idea that the community supplied the basics—food, shelter, and companionship—and left them free of the need to pursue too much success.

Providing shelter has become an almost contradictorily successful business in Good Intent for Curt and Ruth Naser, who run a log-home building business. But their success is under control; they live in a modest log home themselves.

To get there take Road 62118 from Claysville on Route 40. Go west to Road 62120. This will take you across the Danley covered bridge into Good Intent. When you get into town, be careful not to run over the guinea hens. Like the rest of the town, they mean well.

When you're ready to return to the world of getting and spending, if you're seriously interested in fine food and in fine antiques and like the idea of enjoying both together, plan to spend time around Waynesburg. Three miles east of town (take exit 3 off I–79) the ◈ **Greene County Historical Museum,** a mid-Victorian mansion, features thirty-five rooms furnished in antiques of the period; a country store; and collections of pottery, glass, quilts,

7

and Indian and early American artifacts. Also on the grounds is a narrow-gauge steam locomotive. The museum is open May through October, Wednesday to Sunday, for a modest fee. Exact hours of operation change; call (412) 627–3204 for information.

When you're through looking at museum antiques, you might visit ◆**June Stout Antiques** with an eye to buying some good pieces of your own. June's antiques fill most of the rooms in her Federal-style, four-on-four brick home built in 1858, plus seven other buildings, just outside the village of Ruffcreek. June prides herself on selling no "collectibles" but only what fits her definition of true antiques—one-of-a-kind handmade pieces at least one hundred years old. Within the definition she's got everything nameable, from books, vintage clothes, china, and silver to dining tables large enough to seat fifty. She'll show it all to you, for as long as your strength holds up, entertaining you with a running commentary on the antiques, the neighbors, her family, and anything else that comes to mind. "My son says to take a nerve pill when you come in," she jokes.

Inevitably, if you stop at June's, you'll go through the kitchen, where you can't miss her huge parrot, which spends its time alternately sitting atop (and outside) its cage and riding on the back of one of the cats. Somewhere in the house you'll come across the sign her son gave her: THIS IS NOT A MUSEUM. THIS JUNK'S FOR SALE.

"Anything I have bought is for sale," June says, meaning that she doesn't indulge in the habit of some antique dealers of keeping the best pieces she finds for herself. However, if it was given to her as a gift, you probably can't buy it at any price. People call June from all over the country for help in locating hard-to-find pieces. She welcomes business in the shop, but she isn't always home; so while she'll let you in almost any time if she knows you're coming, you definitely should make an appointment before you go. Call (412) 627–6885. To get there take exit 4 off I–79 to Ruffcreek, then go ½ mile north on Route 221.

June says you can see many of the antiques she's found at ◆**Willow Inn,** 6 miles south of Waynesburg in the village of Oak Forest. Willow Inn is an authentically restored 1790 home, furnished mostly in original painted furniture dating from the early 1800s.

Ralph Wilson, who does all the cooking at the inn, restored it himself. The other proprietor, Patrick Verner, who waits on the tables, got frustrated back in 1975 that he couldn't find the kind of primitive paintings he wanted for the inn, so he decided to paint some himself. Guests buy these pictures of village scenes, groups of animals looking slightly pie-eyed, and frolicking children almost faster than Pat can paint them.

Willow Inn offers no printed menu; dinner, which is whatever Ralph decides to offer that night, costs $42 a person. Meals are served seven days a week by reservation at least forty-eight hours in advance. It's worth the money and the planning. Ralph's seven-course meals are imaginative and delicious, plentiful, and not the least bit pretentious. A variety of chocolate soufflés made with milk chocolate, white chocolate raspberry, and coffee flavors are especially intriguing. Everything you taste invites pause to figure out all the flavors. Ralph grew up cooking, always trying to produce something unusual from ordinary ingredients. According to Pat, an uncle of Ralph's once said, "Can't Ralph cook a plain egg?" Apparently he can't, but he makes a mean tomato dumpling soup, wonderful whole-wheat bread, lovely veal with green peppercorns, incredible carrots and strawberries Amaretto, amazing walnut bourbon torte . . . ah, weight watchers, alert! Write Willow Inn at R.D. #4, Oak Forest Road, Waynesburg 15370, call (412) 627–9151, or access the Internet at www.willowinn.com. Pay by cash or check; no credit cards are accepted. To get there, take Route 18 south out of Waynesburg 3 miles to the village of East View. About ½ mile south of East View, take a left on the Oak Forest Road. Go 3 miles to the village of Oak Forest. Willow Inn is the first farm on the right past Oak Forest.

The better part of wisdom warns against driving far after a meal like that. Pat and Ralph recommend staying at ◆ **Log Cabin Bed and Breakfast,** just 6 miles down the road. Jane and Terry Cole welcome you into a restored 1820 colonial log home with three huge guest rooms, furnished with family antiques to be "not fancy, just comfortable," as Jane puts it. The original log cabins themselves are unchanged, though a colonist come to life probably would be surprised by the modern baths and Finnish sauna, even if the Coles' coffee by the fire or lemonade on the porch seemed familiar. Rates include continental breakfast. Payment is by cash or check, no credit cards, and reservations are required (412–451–8521).

As you head north from here, back on I–79, you come to "The City." Pittsburgh isn't off the beaten path, no question. But as cities go, it's more agreeable than most; and with the inter-states—I–79 coming from the north and south, I–76 running east and west—and the controlled-access Parkways 279 and 376, the city is remarkably easy to get into. On your way from the south-ern to the northern part of the state (or vice versa), you can stop to take a look at the city without giving up a whole day.

And Pittsburgh is worth a second look, because it is one of those rare places (once known as "The Smoky City") that has overcome all kinds of industry-induced pollution and renewed itself eco-nomically and environmentally. People who live here are proud of it. Today they call Pittsburgh "The Renaissance City." Because it is built among many hills between the Allegheny and Mononga-hela rivers, the feel of the city is more like that of a country town in the mountains—with more traffic, of course.

If you decide to spend some time here, try to visit at least the Carnegie, the Pittsburgh Zoo, the Carnegie Science Center, and, on the campus of the University of Pittsburgh, the Cathedral of Learning.

The ✦**Carnegie,** at 4400 Forbes Avenue, (412) 622–3131, was made possible by Pittsburgh's famous philanthropist Andrew Carnegie. It reflects the emphasis on the arts in the city. The complex is devoted to a multiplicity of cultural interests, all under one roof. The Carnegie Music Hall seats 2,000 people; this is where most of Pittsburgh's major music organizations per-form. The Carnegie Library is considered one of the best public libraries in the country. The Carnegie Museum of Art features the work of nineteenth- and twentieth-century American artists, Impressionists and post-Impressionists. The Carnegie Museum of Natural History displays Egyptian artifacts, dinosaur skele-tons, and interactive geology exhibits. These are especially pop-ular with children.

The ✦**Pittsburgh Zoo,** at Hill Road, maintains exhibits with more than 6,300 animals in their naturalistic habitats on 75 acres. Habitats include a tropical forest, an aqua zoo (aquarium), an African savanna, and a reptile house. In the rain-forest habitat, endangered species such as gorillas have been assembled. The zoo is open daily from 10:00 A.M. to 6:00 P.M. from Memorial Day to Labor Day, and from 9:00 A.M. to 5:00 P.M. the rest of the time. Closed Thanksgiving and Christmas. Moderate admission fee. Phone (412) 665–3639. To get to the zoo, take the Highland Park exit from Route 28. Go south across the bridge to Butler Road. Follow signs onto Baker Street.

The ◆ **Carnegie Science Center** (locally often called the Buhl Science Center), at One Allegheny Avenue, is full of hands-on exhibits. It advertises itself as an "amusement park for the mind" and looks at everything from cryogenics to robotics. You can manipulate the foundation of a 30-foot water sculpture to play with hydraulics. Miniaturists will like the elaborate miniature railroad and village display. In front of the center, in full scale, the submarine U.S.S. *Requin,* from World War II, gives you a glimpse of what the deep-sea fighting vessels were like. Compared to many of Pittsburgh's long-established attractions, the science center is relatively new, having opened in 1990. This means you can almost certainly find unexpected exhibits added after deadline time when you visit. Yet the place has the vigor of a museum in full maturity. The museum is across from Three-River Stadium's parking lots #1 and #2, to their right. Schedules for the various attractions in the science center vary, as do admission rates. For full details phone (412) 237–3400. Be prepared to respond to an automatic answering touch-tone voice system elaborate enough to be an exhibit in itself!

The ◆ **Cathedral of Learning,** on the campus of the University of Pittsburgh, stands on the quadrangle at the convergence of Bigelow Boulevard, Fifth Avenue, Bellefield Avenue, and Forbes Avenue. Even if you don't want to go inside, take the time to drive by. The beautiful structure is a forty-two-story Gothic stone tower. Deciduous trees and expanses of grass soften the effect. Nineteen "nationality classrooms" are intended to reflect the rich cultural mix of Pittsburgh (and western Pennsylvania). ("Rich cultural mix" is, of course, a public-relations kind of phrase. The people in western Pennsylvania have typically called one another Spaghetti Benders, Cake Eaters, Polka Dancers, etc., based on nationality; they do it matter-of-factly, not with rancor.) As time and mobility continually dilute the ethnic strains, this place is made even more important. Each of the rooms was designed and decorated by people from the countries of the major nationalities established in Pittsburgh. Tour hours vary seasonally, though weekends are the best time to visit. A modest admission fee is

Cathedral of Learning

charged. Phone (412) 624–6000 if you are sufficiently interested in architecture to want to go inside.

For sidewalk browsing, Pittsburgh is developing an area known as **The Strip,** between Smallman and Penn avenues along the Allegheny River. This section was once entirely devoted to wholesale food markets. It's still a great place to find fresh produce, fish, cheese, coffee, and the like, but street artists and small shops have moved in, too, so now you can spend the morning browsing with a pastry in one hand and coffee in the other, buying not only food but also jewelry, pottery, and craft items. And on a permanently anchored barge called **The Boardwalk,** on the river, you'll find restaurants and nightclubs—probably the ultimate in gentrification. Be that as it may, this area is a lot of fun to wander around in.

ALLEGHENY RIVER COUNTRY

Just northeast of Pittsburgh off Route 28 are several special outdoor nature spots. In early May, ◆ **Trillium Trail** delights visiting wildflower enthusiasts. Following an easy ½-mile trail reveals countless thousands of white trilliums blooming on the hillside above a ravine, where, in addition, many labeled wildflowers along the way catch your attention every few steps. You won't be alone here during bloom season, but part of the fun is seeing how many different sorts of people enjoy an unspoiled show of wildflowers. This is a good place to go with children, because the undemanding trail takes a relatively short time to walk. From Route 28, take the Fox Chapel Road exit and drive nearly a mile to Squaw Run Road. Turn left. A mile down the road you will come to a fork in the road. Both choices lead to parking lots for the trail.

Nearby, ◆ **Beechwood Farms Nature Reserve,** which, like Fallingwater, is a property of the Western Pennsylvania Conservancy, has longer and more varied trails. Run by the Audubon Society, the reserve is great for wildflowers, birds, and photography. As suggested by the names of some of the trails, Goldenrod Trail and Violet Trail, spring is a good time to stop here, too. The trails are open from sunup to sundown.

Just before you pick up Goldenrod Trail, you can watch a wind generator in action; farther down the trail Canada geese populate a pond. As you follow the trails into the woods, you'll see many different birds.

The reserve includes a book and gift shop and nature displays, as well as a group of truly enthusiastic volunteers, who keep everything running smoothly. They provide you with maps, information, and advice on where to walk depending on your particular interests. The reserve is open Tuesday through Saturday, 9:00 A.M. to 5:00 P.M. and Sunday 1:00 to 5:00 P.M. To get to the reserve, take the Fox Chapel Road exit north from Route 28. Go nearly a mile. Turn left on Squaw Run Road. Drive just over a mile. Take a left fork to Dorseyville Road. Beechwood Farms is almost 2 miles down the road on the left.

For more information about the reserve write 614 Dorseyville Road, Pittsburgh 15238; phone (412) 963–6100.

OHIO RIVER VALLEY

You can appreciate some more recent history on a trip to ◈ **Old Economy Village,** at Ambridge, less than an hour northwest of Pittsburgh. Old Economy is a preserved village of the old Harmony Society, which was founded in this country when the society's leader, George Rapp, brought a group of his followers from Germany to avoid persecution and live in the promised land. The Harmonites believed that the second coming of Christ was about to happen. They became a communal, celibate society so they would be pure when it did.

Rapp's first settlement, which he called the "First Terrestrial Home," was Harmony, Pennsylvania. The Harmonites turned out to be good makers of cloth as well as craftspeople and farmers, and they produced impressive profits in manufacturing. They established their "Second Terrestrial Home" in Harmony, Indiana, because they needed more land and wanted to be close to a navigable river and western markets. Nobody knows why the group moved again in 1824, but they came back to Pennsylvania to build Economy, 20 miles north of Pittsburgh on the Ohio River, where they quickly established themselves as a successful manufacturing community.

Their beliefs did not suggest that being ready for the New Kingdom meant that they had to give up the niceties of this one. They practiced the "Divine Economy," a melding of their religious principles, economic ideas, and social life. Religion came first in their lives, but their communal lifestyle was not austere. Harmonites ate well, made and drank wine, adorned their furniture, wore silk on Sunday, played music, planted flower gardens, and made money for the community.

The eventual demise of the society, in 1905, happened for several reasons. The followers of George Rapp expected him to lead them into the New Kingdom, so when he died in 1847 without that having happened, the faith of many was seriously shaken. Also, about a third of the society's members had left during an earlier rift. Finally, any celibate group that stops taking in new members and can't give birth to its own obviously lives on borrowed time.

Although when they ran out of members their social and religious experiment stopped working, their canny business sense produced fine furniture, sturdy buildings, beautiful grounds, and many beneficial investments in the nearby towns. It's fascinating to reflect on all this as you tour the village.

You should allow at least half a day for your visit. Not only is the formal tour long (it can take well over an hour), but also you'll want to allow time to look around some more on your own and to browse in the gift shop and gardens. The tour includes the community kitchen, the cabinet and blacksmith shops, the granary, wine cellar, tailor shop, store, great house, and other buildings. You have a lot to see and a lot to think about here.

Tour guides know much about both religious beliefs and the history of the community. When an old object has been placed somewhere it was not originally placed or when restoration somehow deviates from the original structure, the guides will point it out and explain. They do an outstanding job of answering questions.

The village is open Tuesday through Saturday 9:00 A.M. to 4:00 P.M. and Sunday noon to 4:00 P.M. The last tour begins at 3:00 P.M. (Closed Mondays and holidays, except Memorial Day, July 4, and Labor Day.) Moderate rates are charged. For information about daily tours and special events, write Harmonie Associates, Fourteenth and Church streets, Ambridge 15003 or call (412) 266–4500. To get there exit I–79 at Coraopolis and take Route 65 along the Ohio River to Ambridge.

A few minutes north of Rochester, still on Route 65, New

Brighton offers another kind of individual enterprise, the **Lapic Winery Ltd.,** operated by Dennis and Josephine Lapic. The winery is open daily for wine tasting and sales, except on election days and major holidays. Family tours are held on Sundays. The tours include the vineyards as well as the winery, and group tours also include a slide show in the Old Wine Cellar and wine tasting at $3.00 a glass. An appointment is necessary to schedule tours. Call ahead (412–846–2031) to arrange tours, or write 682 Tulip Drive, New Brighton 15066.

A poke and a plum away (poke your head out the car window and you're plum outta town), Beaver, on Route 68 between Routes 51 and 60, has ◆ **Richmond Little Red School,** a one-room schoolhouse used from 1844 until 1950, now restored with many of its original furnishings. A group of local volunteers, some of whom received the first eight years of their elementary education in the redbrick school, got together to put it back into shape. They act as hosts and guides to visitors, answering questions about what it was like to go to school there.

The original bell hangs in place over the door, the pump out front has been painted red to match the brick, and the "functioning" outhouse (not exactly the same as the original but a genuine outhouse, nonetheless) does what outhouses have always done. Because the building gets cold in winter and heats slowly once a fire is built in the potbellied stove, the volunteers prefer not to schedule group tours in the dead of winter. The school is open Sunday from 2:00 to 5:00 P.M. in June, July, and August. Tours may be arranged by appointment. Write Park Road, Beaver 15009 or call (412) 775–1989.

OHIO BORDER

More directly north of Pittsburgh, you'll find ◆ **McConnells Mill State Park,** which has something to appeal to history buffs, geologists, birders, botanists, rock climbers, hunters and fishermen, rafters, and, of course, picnickers. The feature from which the park gets its name is a restored gristmill. A covered bridge dating from 1874 just below the mill is still in use. To get to the mill and bridge, you have to park in a lot near the top of the hill and follow a footpath down. You may take a free guided tour of the mill in the summer or go through on your own.

While you're in the mill, pick up a brochure and a map for the Kildoo nature trail, a 2-mile loop, not as easy as the walks at Trillium Trail and the Beechwood Farms Nature Reserve, but unusual in that a paved area at the beginning of the trail accommodates people confined to wheelchairs. Along the trail, depending on the season, you'll see a variety of evergreens, wildflowers and lichens, and many species of ferns. Also in the park you can study the geological wonders of ❖ **Slippery Rock Gorge,** some 20,000 years old and 400 feet deep, and other rock formations that have been there millions of years. For more information about tours, hunting, and fishing, phone (412) 368–8091. To get there it's easiest to take I–79 40 miles north from Pittsburgh to the Route 422 exit. Go almost 2 miles west on Route 422. A sign indicates a left turn for the park.

Just about fifteen minutes from the park, near the little town of Slippery Rock, on Route 173, are the **Applebutter Inn,** a bed-and-breakfast inn in an old restored farmhouse, and its accompanying restaurant, the **Wolf Creek School Cafe,** in a restored one-room schoolhouse. Here you'll find good food and bucolic accommodations. Just shoot up I–79 to the next exit (Slippery Rock), follow Route 108 7 miles to Route 173, and go right on Route 173 for ¼ mile. The original six-room farmhouse was built in 1844 from bricks made on the premises. From the time it was built until Gary and Sandra McKnight began restoring it, it had housed only the family that built it and one other. The McKnights began restoring it in 1987, uncovering old fireplaces, restoring woodwork, and building on an addition for more guest rooms. There are eleven guest rooms, all furnished with period antiques and fitted with contemporary amenities as well. First-floor rooms have wheelchair access, and one room is especially equipped for the disabled, a rare service in old restored buildings.

When it's nice to be outside, the meadow and the pond where wild geese sometimes stop are pleasant; on less-than-perfect days, the sunroom, with its white wicker furniture and enough houseplants to bring the outdoors in, makes a good place to relax.

The inn serves a gourmet breakfast at the Wolf Creek School Cafe. The old one-room school building that houses this restaurant was moved onto the premises and renovated in the spirit of its original use. Menu specials were written in chalk on the original school blackboards. Offerings include homemade breads and lots of apple dishes, in keeping with the inn's name. The breakfast pizza is one of the most intriguing specialties. The restaurant also serves a nice variety of lunch choices, soups, salads, and sandwiches, with one special "dinner entree" each day. For instance, Lemon-Parmesan Crusted Chicken is a popular favorite. The restaurant is open to inn guests and the public. For more information about the inn, call (412) 794–1844; for information about the restaurant, call (412) 794–1899.

You might want to look around Slippery Rock briefly, if only for its curiosity value. The little town is the home of the former Slippery Rock State Teachers College, now **Slippery Rock State University.** These days it looks pretty much like most college towns, with lots of sundry shops and small eating places. One resident said the recent addition of a McDonald's made the place "big time." If the town's name sounds familiar, it's because, as kind of a joke, many football stadiums in the country add the Slippery Rock scores at the end of their top ten reports on the public-address system. Enough people have been titillated by the name to generate some funny stories about its origin. According to the best story, the Indians named it. Seems one day the Big Chief was standing by the creek and slipped on a rock. "This is a slippery rock," he said, and the rest is history.

Quiet Amish Country

When you drive between Erie and Pittsburgh, the urge is nearly irresistible just to get on I–79 and stay there, unless you have some specific reason to get off. This stretch of I–79 is entirely rural, scenic, fairly lightly traveled, and more pleasant than most interstate trips. But roughly halfway between Erie and Pittsburgh, it's worth taking some time to go both east and west on Route 208. The easterly road goes into Grove City (a pretty little college town), where you can visit ◆ **Wendell August Forge.** Grove City is close to where I–80 and I–79 intersect. From I–79 take exit 31; or from I–80, take exit 3A. Both are clearly marked with signs directing you into Grove City; more signs lead you directly to Wendell August Forge at 620 Madison Avenue. It's like finding a tiny self-contained industry in the middle of a quiet community where everyone else is doing something else. This is one of the few remaining forges in the country that still makes forged aluminum, pewter, bronze, and sterling silver pieces by hand, without any production machinery.

The forge was founded in 1923 by, predictably enough, Wendell August, who discovered that light metals could be made decorative by forging rather than casting them. Originally, the forge produced ornamental gates, grills, tables, and the like, mainly for larger institutional buildings. At the end of each job, Mr. August would present the customer with a small bowl or vase from the forge. These gifts turned out to be so popular that the entrepreneurial Mr. August began producing gift items for sale.

Today the forge is operated by another entrepreneurial businessman, Bill Knecht, who decided to leave the IBM corporate life to run his own business in a small town and in 1978 bought the forge. A team of thirty-five master craftspeople now produce aluminum, bronze, pewter, copper, and sterling silver pieces. A die cutter creates the original die, and then the pieces are hand hammered from the dies. The hammered pieces are colored over the forge fire and then hand finished. No two pieces are ever alike. Visitors are allowed to walk through the shop section of the forge to see the entire process in action and ask the craftspeople questions.

All the items produced at the forge are for sale in the showroom for prices ranging from a few dollars to a few thousand. Plant tours for individuals are available Monday through Saturday 9:00 A.M. to 4:00 P.M.; the showroom is open Monday through Thursday and Saturday, 9:00 A.M. to 6:00 P.M., Friday until 8:00 P.M., and Sunday 9:00 A.M. to 5:00 P.M. The phone number at the forge is (412) 458–8360.

Going west on Route 208 from I–79 takes you to Volant, about 10 miles away from Grove City, and 4 miles farther, New Wilmington, the charming, historic home of **Westminster College.** This is the heart of a refreshingly noncommercial Amish area as well.

The ◆**Candleford Inn Bed and Breakfast,** run by Donna and Morris Green, offers lodging and breakfast to travelers, by reservation. The fact that the inn was mislabeled "Cranford Inn" in an earlier edition of this book did not keep guests from finding and enjoying the place, and it tells you something about the Greens' flexibility that they answered willingly to either name when confused would-be guests came looking for them. The

Greens had lived in the huge old house for some time before they decided to strip it down, restore it, and turn it into a bed-and-breakfast inn. Donna says, "It's not exactly colonial and it's not exactly Victorian. It's 1900s everything." The antiques, milk glass, china, and old photos in the inn are all family pieces, the legacy of parents who never threw away anything. One of the inn's three guest rooms is done in Amish style and features a canopy bed made by a local Amish craftsperson. Guests who stay here are treated to coffee and tea in their rooms to wake up before breakfast. Breakfast is worth waking up for: homemade sweet rolls, homemade granola, and a special blueberry brickle. Asked how he would describe the blueberry brickle, Morris said, "Yum, yum."

Morris points out that the little community of Volant has become "craft country," with more than thirty little shops selling antiques, handmade gifts, candy, and boutique items. Candleford Inn rates are modest. Write Mercer Street, Volant 16156; call (412) 533–4497.

NORTHWESTERN PENNSYLVANIA

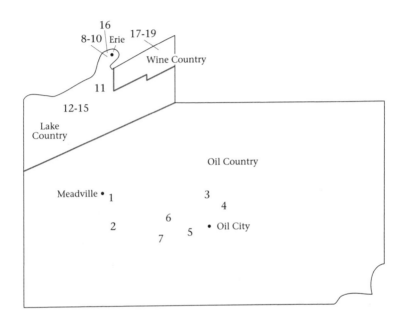

1. Allegheny College
2. Market House
3. Drake Well Park and Museum
4. Pithole
5. Oil Creek and Titusville Railroad
6. Hearts Content Recreation Area
7. Hickory Creek Wilderness
8. Presque Isle State Park
9. Nature Center
10. Ecological Reservation
11. Gull Point Sanctuary
12. East Boat Livery
13. Flagship Niagara
14. Firefighters Historical Museum
15. Erie Historical Museum and Planetarium
16. The Glass Growers
17. Freeport Public Beach
18. Hornby School Museum
19. Lake Shore Railway Museum

Northwestern Pennsylvania

Oil Country

In the northwest part of the state, tucked away in small towns along the way, several places are interesting enough to lure you from the ease of the interstate. Just off I–79 in Meadville, where the zipper (originally called the "hookless fastener") was invented and first produced, ◆**Allegheny College,** one of the oldest colleges west of the Alleghenies, has a good collection of Lincoln memorabilia in the Pelletier Library. Ida Tarbell, one of the first muckrakers, acquired the materials when she wrote an early, extensive biography of the Lincolns; she donated them to her alma mater. Tarbell was one of the college's first female students. She majored in biology because she hoped that she could find God with what she could learn through a microscope. She remained a devoted alumna till she died. The library also has many interesting papers, books, and artifacts related to Miss Tarbell. Two of the college buildings, Bentley Hall and Ruter Hall, are listed on the National Register of Historic Places.

Meadville's historic downtown includes more than a dozen historic buildings that should interest those who care about old architecture. A self-guided tour to historic points in Meadville is available wherever tourist literature is distributed; better yet, pick up the tour brochure at ◆**Market House,** 910 Market Street. This is the commercial and cultural center of the community. The Crawford County Tourist Association office is on the second floor. On the ground floor a farmers' market flourishes, as it has for more than a hundred years. You can pick up a bite to eat at the lunch counter there to hold you over while you shop through the array of produce, flowers, baked goods, handicrafts, cheese, ceramics, and collectibles in the marketplace. Market House is open year-round.

Approximately 30 miles east of Meadville, you can get a fascinating glimpse of the early influence of oil, before Texas or foreign countries even thought of it, in Pennsylvania. Start at Titusville with the ◆**Drake Well Park and Museum,** the site where the *world's* first successful oil well was drilled. The well is topped by a replica of the derrick. The museum contains a detailed history of

Drake Well Park and Museum

the early oil days, including a twenty-five-minute film about how the first well came to be drilled. In the library are thousands of photographs from the early oil days. The library also holds more papers of Ida Tarbell, in this case those related to her famous exposé, *The History of the Standard Oil Company.* Her own family had been involved in the beginnings of the oil industry, and this background pushed her away from science into journalism, writing about oil. Her personal scrapbooks, including clippings of some of her reviews, bring the story down to a personal level quite different from the accounts of history books.

Oil apparently has been generating press and publications for as long as we've been drilling it, because the museum boasts 3,500 books, 1,000 periodicals, and 1,000 newspapers dealing with oil news from the period. There's also a collection of 4,000 glass-plate negatives from the work of John A. Mather, one of the earliest photographers of oil scenes.

The park is ½ mile southeast of Titusville on Route 8. The museum (814–827–2797) is open from 9:00 A.M. to 5:00 P.M. every day, except from November 1 to the end of April, when it is closed all day Monday and until noon Sunday. Closed on major holidays year-round.

A short drive southeast on Route 27 and then south on Route 227 brings you to Plummer, about 1½ miles farther south from which you'll find the ghost town of ❖ **Pithole.** It was an oil boom town in the late 1860s and was abandoned when the oil business fell off. A museum building on the grounds contains a pictorial history of Pithole and artifacts of the area, but by far the most interesting activity here is wandering across the site of the town, where nothing remains but cellar holes, wells, and the depressions of streets. It's a little as it might feel to go to a Texas oil town and find nothing left but grassy mounds of earth where people and businesses used to thrive. You can pick up a walking-tour brochure at the visitor center, open from Memorial Day to Labor Day, Wednesday noon to 5:00 P.M. and Thursday to Sunday 10:00 A.M. to 5:00 P.M. Hours are subject to change. Modest fees are charged to visitors. Call (814) 589–7912 for information.

There are several other ways to see some of the oil country and historic sites while enjoying a respite from highway driving. One is to ride the ❖ **Oil Creek and Titusville Railroad,** sponsored by the Oil Creek Railway Historical Society. The trip, which takes two hours, runs from Titusville to Rynd Farm, 4 miles north of Oil City, passing through the sites of several boom towns and some lovely countryside. You can board at the Drake Well Museum, at the Perry Street Station in Titusville, on the southern end of the trip, at Rynd Farm. The schedule of northbound and southbound trains is complicated, may change without notice, and includes additional trains scheduled for special celebration weeks in the summer; moreover, you need advance tickets to guarantee that you'll have a place on the train. To learn what the schedule will be when you plan your visit, write OC & T RR, P.O. Box 68, Oil City 16301, or call (814) 827–2797 or (814) 676–1733. Ticket prices are moderately high.

If you'd like to make part of the same trip on bicycle, try the 10-mile paved trail along Oil Creek from Petroleum Center to Drake Well Park. The trail is open from 8:00 A.M. to dark.

Enjoy a more amusing kind of history at the **DeBence Antique Music World,** not far away on Route 8, 2 miles south of Franklin. The museum has more than 250 antique music boxes, including a rare Berry Wood, Style A.O.W. Automatic, Orchestra— an automatic player that produces the sounds of thirteen different instruments. Jake and Elizabeth DeBence play all the nickelodeons, band organs, orchestrions, and music boxes, and they provide guided tours of the museum. They also buy and sell other antiques, including lamps, old toys, trains, and furniture. The museum is open from mid-April to late October (depending on the weather) Tuesday to Saturday 10:00 A.M. to 5:00 P.M. and Sunday 12:30 to 5:00 P.M. Call (814) 432–5668 for details; a moderate admission fee is charged.

Right in downtown Franklin you can return to the railroad theme. **The Franklin Depot,** 1215 Railroad Street, serves breakfast, lunch, dinner, and Sunday brunch in a rambling edifice consisting of an old train-station depot and train cars. The kitchen used to be a baggage car. The waiting area and a dining room are in the original station depot. Old dining cars brought in from the New York Central Railroad form the center of more dining rooms. The decor includes a chandelier from Oil City, a row of huge clay piggy banks, the potbellied stove from a caboose, and full-size mannequins in old train uniforms.

The actual station was built in 1866; the restaurant was established in 1985.

Menu offerings include all kinds of breakfast items, from pancakes to Cajun eggs Benedict, a concoction so spicy you may rename it "eggs Benedict Arnold" an hour or so after eating. For lunch you choose from all kinds of burgers, sandwiches, and chicken. Dinners range from prime rib and seafood to pastas and Oriental stir-fry dishes. Beer, wine, and cocktails are available. The restaurant is open Monday through Friday 9:00 A.M. to 8:00 P.M. and Saturday and Sunday 7:00 A.M. to 8:00 P.M. or later. Phone (814) 437–1866.

The town of Franklin itself dates back to 1753, when the

DeBence Antique Music World

French had Fort Machault here. Seven years later the British built Fort Venango. But, as with so much of this part of Pennsylvania, striking oil was what really gave life to the community. It's worth taking a little time to check out the local-history displays in the **Hoge-Osmer House,** at the corner of South Park and Elk streets. Also take a look at the **Venango County Courthouse** at Twelfth and Liberty streets. The courthouse is noted for its unusual architecture. And if you're on Twelfth Street on

Wednesday or Saturday, you can spend some time browsing through the local farmers' market.

You can find all this simply by wandering around town, or you can request a self-guided walking tour at the Franklin Area Chamber of Commerce, 1259 Liberty Street. For further information phone (814) 432–5823.

From this area you can pick up U.S. Route 62 to drive through Oil City to the Allegheny National Forest for some truly off-the-beaten-path travel. Just past East Hickory, at Endeavor, turn right on PA Route 666, heading into the forest. When you get to Truemans you also come to **Fools Creek Store,** perched right by the road, on a curve, surrounded with woods and gardens in a weathered house old enough to look ageless. Here Margaret M. Stamm, proprietor, keeps hours from noon to 5:00 P.M. Saturday and Sunday. You may find her, her sign says, by chance or by appointment the rest of the week. Phone (814) 968–3788. Margaret sells all kinds of kerosene lamps and other small antiques as well as a few kinds of canned soup and stew and crackers (presumably for hunters). She says she is in her eighties, and though she doesn't look it, when she gets to telling you stories about her life and family, you figure she must be. There's no way she could have fit so many events into a lifetime.

From here you can turn around and drive back about ¼ mile, where you'll see a dirt Forest Service road just before you come to Mayburg. This is Robbs Creek Road, also known as Forest Highway 116. Turn left on it. Drive on to Hearts Road and turn left again. In about 2 miles you'll come to ◆**Hearts Content Recreation Area** in the Allegheny National Forest.

Often the dirt-road signs are missing. If you want a surer route, get back to U.S. Route 6, which is 15 miles southwest of Warren. From the Mohawk exit of Route 6, take Pleasant Drive south for 11 miles. At the hard curve turn left onto a gravel road; go south for 4 miles to Hearts Content Recreation Area. Getting lost is no hardship either way, because the area is so beautiful.

The **Allegheny National Forest of Pennsylvania** is one of fifteen national forests in the eastern United States. It is the only national forest in Pennsylvania. It covers nearly 512,000 acres. Hardwoods make up most of the timber: black cherry, yellow poplar, white ash, red maple, and sugar maple. This forest is lumbered as part of maintaining its health. More than 65 million board feet of timber, especially black cherry, are harvested each year. The black cherry is used for fine furniture; much of the rest is used for pulpwood. Hearts Content, one comparatively small area of the entire forestland, has some of the oldest tracts of virgin beech and hemlock forests in the eastern United States.

From Hearts Content Recreation Area you can hike, camp, and picnic. But whatever you do, you must take the scenic walk marked by signs. It is short and easy, and it is one of the loveliest spots in Pennsylvania. The place seems to invite meditation. Streams make light music. The old deciduous trees arch higher than gothic arches, letting through just enough blue sky and sunlight to nurture the growth of ferns, which reach your knees. Pines and hemlocks scent the air, nature's improvement on incense. The forest floor, softened with pine needles and leaves, absorbs enough sound to make the walk seem as quiet as a cathedral. A six-year-old child walking through the area for the first time caught its mystery by asking, "Are we inside or outside?"

The ◆**Hickory Creek Wilderness** is next to the campground. This is 8,570 acres of wilderness. No motorized equipment is allowed. An 11-mile hiking loop takes you through rolling terrain. You will probably see deer and all kinds of birds and small wildlife.

LAKE COUNTRY

The drive from Pittsburgh to Erie takes about two hours on I–79, if you don't stop anywhere along the way to explore; but once you get into Erie County, whatever route you've taken, it's almost like being in a different country. As an Erie resident likes to say, "You can't get more off the beaten path than Erie." The sense comes from the facts that Ohio, Lake Erie, and New York form the western, northern, and eastern borders of the county and that getting to Erie from anywhere in Pennsylvania means driving through miles and miles and miles of woodland and uninhabited countryside. But once you get there, you'll find a lot of fun and history in the area.

Fewer than twenty years ago, suggesting a pleasure trip to Lake Erie would have sounded like a big joke. People had a grim saying: "Dreary Erie, the mistake by the lake." Fish kills kept many of the beaches unpleasant. Snapshots from those years show people standing on the beaches up to their knees in soap suds. Old fishermen who remembered when fish were so plentiful you could catch them with nothing but spaghetti for bait couldn't pull out anything but trash fish. The lake had been pronounced dead. But the problem was actually too much of the wrong kinds of life. Nutrients such as phosphates and nitrates, especially plentiful in agricultural runoff, encouraged excessive growth of algae, which grew so fast that they choked out other forms of plant life and fish life. The process is called *eutrophication.* In bad water where no oxygen can reach the bottom, the only fish that can live are the small pan fish. As Lake Erie deteriorated, only pan fish were surviving.

A massive combined effort by area manufacturing companies, local colleges, state and federal government, and concerned citizens turned things around. The City of Erie has improved its sewage disposal system. The Department of Health tests for harmful bacteria regularly. Industries treat their wastes so they won't hurt the lake. Colleges run ecology projects, continuously monitoring the state of the water. At least one Erie councilman pilots his boat, at cost, for the monitoring teams.

Game fish began returning to the waters. The city celebrated, with big headlines in the newspaper, when the first coho salmon was caught after the long empty spell. Perhaps part of the success story comes from the central role that Lake Erie plays in the lives of the people who live there. Hundreds of people go to the public dock in the city every day, if not to fish, at least to check out conditions. Adults who've lived here all their lives talk about having gone out fishing every morning before they went to school or every evening after school; they do the same today with their own children. This spirit affects what it feels like to visit the lakeshores. The passion is contagious.

Among the most ardent fishers are many members, including the past prioress, of the community of Erie Benedictine Sisters, whose main house is on East Lake Road. The sisters get out in boats of varying reliability at the end of many long days to relax with nets and poles. They've developed expertise in all the ways you can cook the fish that come from the lake, including a favorite recipe given them by an old fisherman, which involves baking coho salmon in a combination of mushrooms, French dressing, and Parmesan cheese. The sisters certainly will talk about their vocations and ministries, about religious life, about helping the needy, and so on, but they're also probably the best people around to consult if you want to talk fishing.

The best place to begin learning about Erie and the lake is ✤ **Presque Isle State Park.** If you remember your French, you know that *Presque Isle* means "almost an island." One of the most remarkable places in Pennsylvania, it offers enough to keep you busy for weeks. It's a 3,200-acre peninsula extending from the City of Erie into Lake Erie. Interestingly, the combined effects of erosion on one side and sand deposits on the other change the peninsula's shape and location noticeably, not in thousands of years, but in just a few. The ✤ **Nature Center** in the park displays maps showing the changes. It's estimated that the peninsula has moved about ½ mile east in the past hundred years. Of course, that doesn't make it any harder to find. Nearly 5 million people visit Presque Isle in a good year. Yet if you avoid the peak summer swimming season, it's possible to walk for hours along the beaches and in the woods without seeing another human being.

For naturalists part of the attraction is the area's nearly 300 species of birds and 500 species of ferns and flowering plants. Two undeveloped areas, the ✤ **Ecological Reservation** and ✤ **Gull Point Sanctuary,** are a naturalist's dream. The best way to get acquainted with the possibilities is to study the displays and literature in the Nature Center, where you'll also find less demanding exhibits, such as those of butterflies and ducks, for children. But children are more likely to want to head for the beaches, where the surf is usually high enough to be interesting without getting so rough in good weather as to be dangerous. At the ✤ **East Boat Livery,** you can rent rowboats, canoes, and motorboats. The park is open from dawn to dusk. For more details about winter-sports concessions, guided nature tours, movies, and lectures, as well as Nature Center hours, phone (814) 833–0351. The number for the boat livery is (814) 838–3938. To get to the peninsula from I–79, take the Twenty-sixth Street exit, turn left, and continue to Route 823, which is Peninsula Drive. From Erie go west on West Twelfth Street to Peninsula Drive.

For boating on a grander scale, in the City of Erie, visit the restored ✤ **Flagship Niagara,** one of three American warships surviving from the War of 1812. The *Niagara* commemorates the

Lighthouse at Presque Isle State Park

victory on September 10, 1813, when nine American ships defeated the British fleet on Lake Erie. Visiting her used to be an inland proposition; but now that the restoration is more complete, the ship has been commissioned and is back in the water, in fully operable sailing condition. She is berthed at the foot of Holland Street in Erie, where plans for a bay-front museum are in the works. The *Niagara* is the tallest tall ship on the Great Lakes and is now the official flagship of Pennsylvania.

The restoration process has been almost as dramatic as the events that made the old ship important in the first place. Her restoration called for skills not widely found in the United States,

31

to season and shape the pine and fir, to make the sails, and to forge the custom metal parts used in the rigging. The program involved teaching some of these historical maritime crafts to young men and women of the Pennsylvania Conservation Corps to create a full-sized work crew. The *Niagara* is administered by the Pennsylvania Historical and Museum Commission. Usually, the ship is open for tours, which take an hour or so, from the beginning of April to September 1, Tuesday through Saturday 9:00 A.M. to 4:00 P.M. and Sunday noon to 5:00 P.M. Sometimes, however, the ship is away visiting other sites. To be sure it's going to be there when you are in Erie, phone (814) 452–2744. Moderate admission fees are charged.

Another action-oriented display is the ◆ **Firefighters Historical Museum** at 428 Chestnut Street, which is in the old #4 Erie Firehouse. It contains more than 1,300 items of fire-department memorabilia, including old uniforms and equipment and an 1830 hand pumper. The museum is open May through August, 10:00 A.M. to 5:00 P.M. on Saturday and 1:00 to 5:00 P.M. on Sunday. From September through October the museum is open from 1:00 to 5:00 P.M. Saturday and Sunday. Call (814) 456–5969.

Also in the city, ◆ **Erie Historical Museum and Planetarium,** housed in a twenty-four-room mansion from the late 1800s, at 356 West Sixth Street, has exhibits on regional and maritime history, including the Battle of Lake Erie. In other rooms are changing exhibits from the museum collections, decorative arts, and period rooms with outstanding woodwork and stained glass. The planetarium, in the mansion carriage house, re-creates the movements of the sun, moon, planets, and stars. The museum is open Tuesday through Sunday, 1:00 to 5:00 P.M.; the planetarium showings are Saturday at 2:00 P.M., Sunday at 2:00 P.M. and 3:00 P.M., and Tuesday through Friday at 2:00 P.M. Additional hours are scheduled for the museum and planetarium in the summer; call (814) 871–5790.

Although shopping usually isn't what you'd consider an off-the-beaten-path experience, you'll find a stop at ◆ **The Glass Growers** worth some time if you're interested in fine American crafts, arts, and sculptures. Downstairs, this store, not far from the inner city at 701 Holland Street, carries all kinds of contemporary jewelry, studio pottery, carvings, and textile items made by American crafters across the country. Upstairs you'll find fine arts and sculptures for sale, crafted mostly by local and regional artists and displayed in a bright, spacious setting. These upstairs displays change several times a year. The store is *not* a co-op, but a business reflecting the tastes and marketing savvy of the two women owners who attend major crafts markets across the country each year to find material for the shop. The shop is open Monday through Saturday 10:00 A.M. to 5:00 P.M.; (814) 453–3758. Their offerings have proved sufficiently popular to warrant opening a smaller satellite store at Village West, a shopping center with a New England-style setting on Twenty-sixth Street. To get there take the West Twenty-sixth street exit off I–79. Call the main store for more details.

WINE COUNTRY

Continuing east for about 13 more miles brings you to the little rural town of North East, home of four wineries and some interesting historic sites. From Route 5, Route 89 runs down to the ❖ **Freeport Public Beach** on Lake Erie. North East is also just a few minutes drive on Route 89 from I–90, if you are not coming from the City of Erie. Driving along the countryside here, you'll see acres and acres of vineyards. Lake Erie's wine region stretches about 100 miles along the coast, extending only about 5 miles inland. Wine grapes flourish here because the lake creates a microclimate in which cold spring winds off the lake keep the plants from budding too early and being vulnerable to frost. In the summer lake breezes cool the vineyards and keep the air circulating; in the fall the stored summer warmth from the lake delays frost. Because the lake once was much larger and has receded, the soils along the shore are especially fertile.

While you're in North East, stop at the ❖ **Hornby School Museum,** at 10000 Colt Station Road (Route 430) to visit the restored one-room schoolhouse in the style of the 1870s. With a reservation you can arrange to experience the kind of lessons that would have been part of a typical school day. The school is open Sunday from May through October, 1:00 P.M. to 5:00 P.M. and by appointment. Call (814) 725–5680 for more information.

More fun than school, perhaps, ❖ **Lake Shore Railway Museum,** at Wall and Robinson streets, still has a lot to teach. Two children cried all the way there one morning because they hate museums, but at 5:00 P.M. attendants had to chase the kids out of the train cars to close up. The museum displays historical railroad items from the nineteenth and twentieth centuries, ranging from dining-car china to signaling devices. Outside the museum, which is in a station house by the tracks, you may tour a caboose and railroad cars on the siding—a Pullman sleeping car, diner, freight car, coach, baggage car, and caboose. The wooden caboose is kept as it used to be when it was in service, with a stove and cooking area. In front of the station is an old fireless steamer locomotive, built in Erie in 1937. The schedule of the museum varies with the season and includes some special holiday events, so it is important to call ahead for specifics. Phone (814) 825–2724.

CENTRAL PENNSYLVANIA

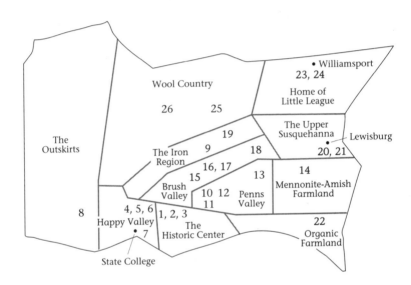

- Williamsport
23, 24
Home of
Little League

Wool Country

26   25

The Upper
Susquehanna   Lewisburg
20, 21

The
Outskirts

19

The Iron   9   18
Region
16, 17
15   13   14
Brush   Mennonite-Amish
Valley   10 12   Penns   Farmland
11   Valley

8   4, 5, 6 1, 2, 3
Happy Valley   The   22
• 7   Historic Center   Organic
Farmland

State College

1. Duffy's Tavern
2. Pennsylvania Military Museum
3. Boal Mansion and Museum
4. Tavern Restaurant
5. All-American Rathskeller
6. Corner Room
7. The Earth and Mineral
   Sciences Museum
8. Eutaw House
9. Curtin Village
10. The Whistle Stop Restaurant
11. Sweet Annie Herbs, Inc.
12. Woodward Cave
13. Woodward Inn
14. Mifflinburg Buggy Museum

15. Penn's Cave
16. Fisher's Harness Shop
17. Madisonburg Bake Shop
18. Brush Valley Greenhouse
19. Rebersburg Post Office
20. Packwood House Museum
21. Colonial Candlecrafters
22. Walnut Acres
23. Peter J. McGovern Little
    League Baseball Museum
24. Reighard House Bed and
    Breakfast Inn
25. The Woolrich Store
26. Cohick's Trading Post

CENTRAL PENNSYLVANIA

THE HISTORIC CENTER

The long-standing joke about central Pennsylvania, especially Centre County, has been that it is equally inaccessible from all points. You must drive several miles in any direction before you come to a major city.

One of the most pleasant sections to visit for a combination of scenery, good food, and historic interest is the Village of Boalsburg, home of the first Memorial Day ceremonies, 3 miles east of State College on Business Route 322. The town was originally a stagecoach stop at the foot of Tussey Mountain; but until the early 1960s, when many area residents became increasingly interested in historic restoration and preservation, the town didn't seem to be much but deteriorating, albeit historic, old houses, cheap rentals for students from nearby Pennsylvania State University. Today virtually all the houses have been restored to picture-book prettiness; specialty shops occupy the fine old buildings on the historic diamond; and ◆ **Duffy's Tavern,** once an 1819 stagecoach tavern, now furnished with antiques, serves steaks, seafood, drinks, and at lunch, a good bean soup. Its atmosphere is unique in that it manages to be both a local bar and a place for gracious dining. It's worth noting that Duffy's history was part of the tavern's ambience long before such emphasis became a national rage. Duffy's is open for lunch 11:30 A.M. to 2:00 P.M. and for dinner 5:00 to 10:00 P.M. Monday through Saturday. Hours on Sunday are 1:00 to 9:00 P.M. Phone (814) 466-6241.

Cross Route 322 to visit the ◆ **Pennsylvania Military Museum,** where exhibits and collections illustrate Pennsylvania's participation in wars from the French and Indian War through World War II. The displays include collections of artifacts from the French and Indian War, dioramas depicting battles of the War for Independence and the War of 1812, and uniforms and equipment from the Mexican and Civil wars. But by far the most spectacular exhibit is the life-sized reproduction of part of a World War I battlefield in France, complete with uniformed "soldiers," trenches, cannon, tank, and truck, through which visitors walk, eerily surrounded by simulated artillery flashes and battle sounds. The museum is open weekdays except Monday from 9:00 A.M. to 5:00 P.M. and Sunday noon to 5:00 P.M. Closed on some holidays. Phone (814) 466–6263. Modest admission charged.

Outside the museum the 28th Division Shrine, begun by Colonel Theodore Boal and fellow members of the 28th Division Officer's Club, memorializes the men of Pennsylvania's 28th Division in World War I. A broad expanse of lawn and some picnic facilities make this a pleasant area to rest or let children run.

Directly across Route 322, on old 322, the ◆ **Boal Mansion and Museum** and the **Christopher Columbus Family Chapel** offer fascinating glimpses of the acquisitions and lives of the Boal family. The mansion was built partly by David Boal in 1789 and finished by his son, David, for whom Boalsburg is named, and finally enlarged by Colonel Theodore Davis Boal in 1898. In these consecutive changes it grew from an early stone cabin to its current grandeur. Inside are fine woodwork and mantels, early American and European furniture, art, china, glass, and silver—the accumulation of nine generations of Boal family furnishings. The chapel belonged to the Columbus family in Spain. The Boal family imported it to Pennsylvania in 1919. In addition to sixteenth- and seventeenth-century woodwork and artwork, the chapel displays church equipment—ancient vestments, chalices, large candlesticks, and statues. The most unusual part of the display is two large pieces of the True Cross, with an Episcopal letter certifying its history. Other buildings on the property contain varied American, French, and Spanish military and domestic relics, some dating from medieval times. The site is open every day except Monday. Hours vary seasonally. The admission fee is moderate. For more details write Curator, Columbus Chapel–Boal Museum, Boalsburg 16827 or call (814) 466–6210.

In a more contemporary mode, if you're in the area on a Tuesday from mid-June through October, you can browse through the **Boalsburg Farmer's Market's** produce, plants, and baked goods, then return to Route 322 to eat at **The Boalsburg Steak House,** which, though not historic, is a long-time tradition and favored eating place among locals. You can't miss it because of the larger-than-life bull on the roof. When the bull first went up, a dozen or so years ago, it immediately became a local joke, and stealing it has been an occasional prank. It's now so much a part of the landscape that The Boalsburg Steak House uses it as part of its advertising logo. The steakhouse serves more than twenty different cuts and sizes of steak, along with seafood and a salad bar. The restaurant (814–466–6251) has complete bar service and is open Monday through Saturday 4:30 to 9:30 P.M., Sunday 3:00 to 8:30 P.M.

HAPPY VALLEY

The main campus of the Pennsylvania State University is at State College, a town that takes its name from days in 1874 when the Agricultural College of Pennsylvania became the Pennsylvania State College. The area is known as "Happy Valley." It tells you something about the place to know that although much confusion comes from the fact that Pennsylvania State University's address is University Park, and few outsiders understand that State College is the name of the town *around* the university, residents have steadfastly refused to change the name of the town. It has too much traffic and too many people to be considered a scheduled getaway, but because of the influence of the university and the kinds of people who are attracted to such places, spending time here can be fun, especially if you avoid football season. The town and university are isolated in rural countryside. Moreover, the location is central to many other interesting spots. To experience the long-standing traditions of the town, you need to dine at the Tavern Restaurant, hoist a beer at the All American Rathskeller or the Post House Tavern, spend the night at the Nittany Lion Inn, and breakfast at The Corner Room, preferably in a window seat.

The ◆ **Tavern Restaurant** was opened by a Penn State graduate who didn't want to leave town. For years it was the only "nice" place to go for a special dinner. It was a favorite with students, who ordered the famous Tavern spaghetti for a dollar, and with faculty, who could afford the steaks and chicken. Even though State College now has many good restaurants, the Tavern remains a nostalgic favorite with local residents and visiting alumni. It's the one restaurant that still feels tweedy and slightly academic. Many of the waiters and waitresses are students; many of the patrons are faculty and long-time residents. The spaghetti is now five or six times that early price, but dinners are still moderately priced. Originally, only beer could be served in State College, but the Tavern now has complete bar service and a cocktail lounge. It is open for dinner 5:00 to 10:00 P.M. daily except Sunday, when it closes at 8:00 P.M. You'll find it on southbound State Route 26, 220 East College Avenue; call (814) 238–6116 for more information.

The ◆**All-American Rathskeller,** 108 South Pugh Street, is just "the Skeller" to people who go there. Only a half block from the wall of campus, it's been a college watering hole since 1933. Generations of students, local ex-students, faculty, and friends of all these have met around the huge booth tables regularly, giving themselves names such as "The Friday Frolic Club," and ordering "a couple a rocks," meaning two pony-sized bottles of Rolling Rock beer, always at a special price. People who check such things claim that the same graffiti has been on the bathroom walls since 1933. Call (814) 237–3858 for information.

Although students do go to **Stoney's Post House Tavern,** located next to the railroad tracks at 45 North Atherton Street, it is more a gathering place for older working people. As for food, the Post House specializes in standard American fare. The atmosphere is just plain bar, but it's friendly and it's got character.

The ◆**Corner Room,** in the old State College Hotel at the corner of Allen Street and College Avenue, where the campus mall meets College Avenue, is a sort of hub and meeting point for town and campus people. It's *the* spot for breakfast, especially for a Corner Room sticky bun. Because the building is on the corner, seating along two long walls looks directly onto the sidewalks, where breakfasters and passersby openly watch each other. If you're there around 10:00 A.M. most days, you'll probably see a handsome, white bearded gentleman who looks a lot like Arthur Treacher sitting at a small inside booth, writing. Gil Abert has been writing (and greeting friends) in the Corner Room for so long he's become part of the tradition. If you speak to him, he'll certainly respond and charm you with his erudition.

It's easy to leave from here to go sightseeing on the Penn State campus, which begins just across the street. Among the possibilities, two are special. ◆**The Earth and Mineral Sciences Museum** in the Steidle Building on Pollock Road exhibits minerals, fossils, and gemstones as well as paintings showing the development of the mineral industries in Pennsylvania. The

39

exhibit highlight is a display of fluorescent minerals where the viewer pushes buttons to light them and show how they react. The museum is open Tuesday through Friday 9:00 A.M. to 5:00 P.M. and Saturday and Sunday 1:00 to 5:00 P.M. It is closed Monday. Farther back on the campus, **Ag Hill** has entertained countless children with its animal barns, deer pens, and creamery ice-cream cones. For adults the flower gardens are a delight in blooming season. Also, as you walk up the mall from College Avenue onto the center of campus, you'll pass the Penn State obelisk—a tall spire built of stone samples from all over Pennsylvania. According to campus legend, it will fall if a virgin walks by.

Back in the town proper, among the myriad changing and student-oriented shops, at 132 South Allen Street, **Aurum/Goldsmiths,** a second-floor sales gallery featuring the work of local goldsmiths in silver, gold, and other metals, offers an appealing collection of contemporary, handcrafted jewelry. They are open regular business hours, Monday through Saturday; call (814) 237–1566 for more information.

THE OUTSKIRTS

While you're in the State College–Boalsburg area, you might want to plan dinner one evening at the ◆ **Eutaw House,** a long-established restaurant in an old colonial inn built in 1823. It's the kind of place to go to for a special occasion. Part of its charm is that if you make a reservation in advance, you can arrange private dining for even as few as two. The menu features aged beef and gourmet seafood. Cocktails and wine are available, and there are eight beers on tap. The Eutaw House (814–364–1039) is in Potters Mills, 13 miles east of State College, at the intersection of Routes 322 and 144. There's nothing else around, so going there really is a separate excursion. Hours are 11:00 A.M. to 10:00 P.M. daily.

An outdoor area worth investigation on the other side of State College is **The Barrens** and **Scotia Pond,** 4 miles west on Route 322. The Shawnee Indians gave it the name because nothing much grows in the sandy acid clay except scrub oak and blueberries. The site is interesting because the life that does persist here includes a number of rare and endangered species, such as the rare buck moth, as well as deer, grouse, and wild turkeys.

Indeed, unless you have a bulletproof suit, it's better to avoid The Barrens during hunting season. Now protected State Game Land, this is the last barren left in Pennsylvania. Much of the adjacent area also was known as barrens less than half a century ago, when teenagers favored it as a place to go and watch the "submarine races" at night. That adjacent area is now a fully established housing development about thirty years old, in which the scrub oak defied naturalists' gloomy predictions of death and instead grew tall enough to make the place overly shady. Scotia Pond and the clay pits in The Barrens attract visitors because of an abundance of wildlife and wildflowers as well as some historic interest, since it is the site of an iron-ore mine built by Andrew Carnegie in the 1800s. The most interesting single feature of the area, however, is probably its freakishly cold temperatures. The ground here absorbs cold, so in winter temperatures may drop to as low as thirty or forty degrees below zero, regardless of the weather in the surrounding area. Even in summer temperatures can be as much as thirty degrees lower than those elsewhere in the region. To get there turn onto Scotia Road from Route 322 and go slightly less than a mile.

THE IRON REGION

Milesburg, a community of about 1,500 people just off I–80 where it is joined by Route 220, isn't particularly close to anything, but it's worth a little time to drive there from State College or to stop off when you're crossing the state on I–80 to visit ◆ **Curtin Village.** This is an old iron village that has gradually been restored so that you can visit the buildings that were part of the original complex.

In this part of the country, ironmasters ruled their villages like monarchies, and, while some must have been benevolent, the old books are full of stories of their tempers and cruelty. One of the worst stories is of an ironmaster becoming angry with his dogs and in a rage driving them into the burning furnace. At this particular site the ironmaster was Roland Curtin. His family home, **Curtin Mansion,** a fourteen-room random fieldstone house in the late Empire style, has been restored and furnished as closely as possible to the way it was when he lived in it in the mid-1800s. On the circular staircase inside, you can see where

Eagle Furnace

generations of Curtins have worn the treads concave. Curtin is still a well-known family name in the area, so much information and history have been available. Also restored are the blacksmith shop, forge, furnace, company store, and railway station. There are a number of log homes in which ironworkers used to live. One was still occupied by an elderly worker until just a few years ago.

A unique feature of the village is that it remained in the Curtin family from 1810 to 1921, when **Eagle Furnace** "blew out." This was the last cold-blast charcoal iron furnace to operate in the United States. Restoration of the home began when the H. L. Curtin family presented the home to the Roland Curtin Foundation for one dollar.

Guided tours include information about Centre County ironmasters and the role of the iron industry in area development, as well as much information about the Curtin family and how the village operated. It is open Wednesday through Saturday 10:00 A.M. to 4:00 P.M. and Sunday 1:00 to 5:00 P.M. from Memorial Day to October. During October hours are 1:00 to 5:00 P.M. Saturday and Sunday. Moderate admission charged. Call (814) 355-1982. Curtin is 3 miles northeast of I–80 from exit 23 on State Route 150.

PENNS VALLEY

From Boalsburg, Route 45 meets Route 322, taking you east to Centre Hall and Old Fort. Sometimes Centre Hall makes the national news as the home of the **Grange Fair,** a true farmers' fair held every year at the end of August that has reached gigantic proportions without losing the qualities that make it unique. In its early days the farmers called Grange Fair "picnic" because they congregated mainly to share food and companionship. Somebody brought some canned goods to show off and then some livestock and one season somebody decided to pitch a tent, thus avoiding a long ride home at the end of the day. The idea caught on. Grange Fair now lasts about a week and many farmers live in tents on the far side of the fairgrounds. There's also a section for campers, but it's in the tent city that you see the most facsinating sights. People bring refrigerators, stoves, beds, even televisions to furnish their tents. In fact, it's not uncommon for a farmer to have a special lot of furnishings reserved just for Grange Fair, and in the day or so before its opening, the roads into Center Hall are full of pickup trucks loaded with everything a family needs to live at the fair for a week. You can be pretty sure you won't find any newcomers to the area in those tents—there's been a waiting list for the tent sites for years, and, typically, occupancy is passed from one generation in a family to the next. This is dairy country so not everybody sleeps at the fair every night; somebody has to go home and milk the cows! Family members often take turns with the chores so that they all get to spend some extended time at the fair.

In addition to the tent city and the R-V campers, Grange Fair has all the traditional trappings of a country fair: food concessions, rides, games, exhibits of needlework, baked goods, produce, and livestock, with blue and yellow ribbons crowning the best in each category.

But you don't have to be in town for the fair to appreciate Centre Hall. This town remains a rural delight even though it's thriving economically in its mountaintop, cross-road location. The old train station has been restored, and the station building itself is now the home of ◆ **The Whistle Stop Restaurant** on the corner where the tracks meet Pennsylvania Avenue (Route 144) between Routes 192 and 45. You can't miss the building; it's been painted red. A caboose and dining car have been restored (and painted even brighter red), too, and the restaurant may eventually expand into even more restored cars. The restaurant serves sandwiches, soups, and salads for lunch and beef, broiled or fried seafood, and, on Thursday nights, barbecued ribs and chicken for dinner. Wednesday night is Central Pennsylvania night when the feature is usually chicken and waffles. One of the nicest places to sit in good weather is in the large screened-in deck. The restaurant is open Tuesday through Thursday 11:00 A.M. to 8:00 P.M., Friday and Saturday 11:00 A.M. to 9:00 P.M., and Sunday 11:00 A.M. to 7:00 P.M. Call (814) 364–2544 for more information.

Next door, the **Station Master's House,** a white and brown turn-of-the-century home, has been turned into a co-op where you can shop for local crafts, collectibles, and antiques. Nine rooms on two floors contain everything from local pressed flower art and handmade quilts to a good collection of rubber stamps, wood toys, handsewn children's clothes, and small antiques. One room is filled with dried and silk floral arrangements as well as bunches of flowers for you to arrange yourself. And, reflecting current popular taste, there are lots of candles and angels. The Station Master's House is open Tuesday through Friday 11:00 A.M. to 5:00 P.M., Saturday 11:00 A.M. to 8:00 P.M., and Sunday noon to 5:00 P.M.

One of the most colorful places in Centre Hall is ◆ **Sweet Annie Herbs, Inc.,** which is located at 233 South Pennsylvania Avenue near the entrance to the fairgrounds. Sweet Annie goes back a couple of decades at least. In the early years she had an herb farm and shop in Tusseyville, not too far from Centre Hall, and was known by the local kids as "Herb Annie." Well before herbs became the big deal they are today, local people took a lively interest in what she was doing. After a rain the kids would say, "I wonder if Herb Annie is out weeding today?" And another woman fretted repeatedly, "She can't keep up with those weeds. She's got to start using mulch."

The *Sweet* Annie moniker is the direct result of the herb of the same name taking over a large area in front of the house in Centre Hall. When it's in full bloom the whole town smells like it. The house is filled with the trappings of Anne's mail-order business, selling medicinal herbs and books, and everything that goes with her frequent appearances on talk radio and sometimes television. The shop is in the barn behind the house. Wood-chip paths wind through herb gardens past a lily pond back toward the store. A sign invites visitors to "take any path," which somehow always makes people smile. Inside you're greeted with a huge array of dried flowers and herbs, potpourri, health products, local honey, handmade throws, decorative items, books, and, as Annie puts it, "anything else that will please your senses." There are tables and chairs at which you can sit and sip tea and chat while you take it all in. The shop is open seven days a week from 10:00 A.M. to 5:00 P.M. Call (800) 995–HERB for more information.

From here you can take two of the most scenic, picturesque, and interesting drives in the state. One is from Centre Hall to Lewisburg on Route 192; the other is from Old Fort, just outside Centre Hall, to Lewisburg on Route 45. Because the two roads parallel each other, to enjoy them both you must backtrack or make a loop. Either way, it's worth the time. Information here is given to proceed from Centre Hall and Old Fort to Lewisburg; you can easily reverse the directions for either trip. Route 45 is the more heavily traveled road and carries some truck traffic, but it's a good road and easy driving. Route 192 is less traveled, more winding, slower, and takes you through a number of charming villages and an area of Amish farms and small shops, in addition to Raymond B. Winter State Park.

Driving from Old Fort east about half an hour on Route 45, you'll find Millheim, a living farming town with some lovely old houses along or near the main street, which is Route 45.

No more than a mile down the road, you'll pass through the little village of Aaronsburg, about which a book once was written because it was founded as a community where people of differing religions intended to coexist in harmony. Nobody could have foreseen that the tolerance would eventually be called upon to extend also to the Amish, who have migrated into the area. It's worth driving slowly through this little town because it is so perfectly kept, with its old homes in such fine repair you feel as though you're moving through a scene from a postcard.

Approximately 5 miles farther you'll come to Woodward, where ◆ **Woodward Cave,** one of the largest stalagmite caves in the state, offers hour-long guided walking tours through the five rooms of the cavern. Unlike most such attractions, this one accommodates wheelchairs. To give you an idea of the size of this cave, when a concert was held in the fourth room one Christmas, it was attended by more than 400 people, and there was room for them all to be seated. Take a sweater even in the summer—the temperature is always forty-eight degrees. It is open 9:00 A.M. to 7:00 P.M. from March 15 to May 15 and 10:00 A.M. to 5:00 P.M. Labor Day to November 15. Rates are $10.00 for adults and $5.00 for children ages 5 to 15. Under 5 are free. Call (814) 349–9800.

If you like the placidity of the Woodward area well enough to want to hang around, you could stay at the ◆ **Woodward Inn,** an 1814 Georgian stone bed-and-breakfast with seven guest rooms available weekends. It is furnished with four generations of family antiques from Germany and Pennsylvania. Breakfast usually includes something like Pennsylvania Dutch shoofly pie or a crumb cake. The rooms do not have telephones or televisions, and some of the rooms share baths. In earlier days this inn did not serve dinner, but that has changed with the arrival of Eric and Claudia Sarnow. The inn's dining room, **The Hummingbird Room,** features the creations of Eric, who worked at Le Bec Fin in Philadelphia until he succumbed to the lure of the woods and relocated in Woodward. Claudia, his wife, runs the dining room. The cuisine reflects the French influence but, Eric says, is special because he cooks with an abundance of fresh local produce. This is no small thing: soil in this area is rich and fertile, so a cabbage or tomato or bean grown here bursts with flavor. This means Eric has the best raw ingredients when he begins, and he's got the good sense to respect that goodness. Call (814) 349–8118.

MENNONITE-AMISH FARMLAND

Your next stop will also be a step back in time at **Mifflinburg.** It dates from the end of the American Revolution. The old homes have been restored, painted with an eye to historic authenticity, and buffed to a Victorian perfection that probably exceeds their original state. In the 1800s Mifflinburg became the "buggy capital" of the country, producing more buggies per capita than any other place in the country. At one time as many as twenty different buggy and sleigh factories were going full tilt in the village. One of them, the Heiss Carriage Works, at 523 Green Street, survives today as the ◆ **Mifflinburg Buggy Museum.**

The story of this museum's success is a great testimony to the community spirit of the Mifflinburg townspeople. At the time of the American Bicentennial, they wanted to do something commemorating their town's history. The Heiss buggy works had been abandoned forty years earlier and locked up. The people decided to buy the house, shop, and repository from the family; restore them as a museum; and offer guided tours, all with community volunteers. When they opened up the main shop, they found it looking as though workers had walked off expecting to return the next day. All the equipment and tools were lying where they had last been used. A lunch pail and half a box of shredded wheat still sat on a workbench. Volunteers have restored the home, with most of its original, modest furnishings intact, and put the shop and repository back into operating condition. Demonstrations of the entire buggy-making process and a chance to go through the house are part of the tour. Many of the same people who worked on the restoration guide the tours; no one here is ever bored and slick, reciting from memorized spiels. An added fillip is that some of the people taking the tour with you may be Mennonites or Amish from the area, people for whom buggies are still an important part of life. The museum is open Saturday and Sunday 1:00 to 5:00 P.M. (the last tour begins at 4:40 P.M.) May through mid-September. Two special events are annual Buggy Days on Saturday and Sunday of Memorial Day weekend and Christmas at the Heiss House the first Sunday of December. Admission is $2.00. Call (717) 966–1355.

BRUSH VALLEY

A couple of miles back down the mountain to Centre Hall, begin your trip east on Route 192 with a stop at ◆ **Penn's Cave.** This is too popular an attraction to be considered undiscovered, but it's a unique cave worth being in the company of tourists to see. You tour this limestone, all-water cavern by boat. Geologically, the cave was the bed of a shallow sea millions of years ago. Today the interior of the cavern is carved by the water into colorful stalagmites and stalactites that resemble familiar forms—dragons and the Statue of Liberty, for instance. In legend the Seneca Indian princess, Nitanee, and her French lover were thrown into the cave to die for defying Indian custom. Historically, it is known that Indians and explorers took shelter in the dry rooms of the cave. Other attractions at Penn's Cave are short airplane rides to see the farmland from the air, a wildlife sanctuary, and a shop featuring antiques and items made in Pennsylvania. In a natural den near the cavern, Boomer, a North American mountain lion, roars at visitors. Penn's Cave is open February 15 to May 31 and September, October, and November, daily from 9:00 A.M. to 5:00 P.M., and in June, July, and August, daily 9:00 A.M. to 7:00 P.M. In December it is open weekends only, 11:00 A.M. to 5:00 P.M. Rates are moderately high. Airplane rides cost $16. Special rates are available for combined cave and flight tickets. For more information call (814) 364-1664.

From here the drive on Route 192 is through rural valleys. More accidents are caused by deer than by other drivers. Be careful. It will probably take you about fifteen minutes to get from Centre Hall to Madisonburg. Following the sign turn off Route 192 onto the little road that takes you back into the village. On your left ◆ **Fisher's Harness Shop,** owned and operated by Amish and lit with gas lanterns, sells and repairs harnesses for area Amish and also sells a variety of tack for regional horsemen and horsewomen. For customers not involved with large animals, the shop has decorative sheepskins, boots, shoes, and assorted other leather goods. It is open Monday through Saturday 8:00 A.M. to 5:00 P.M.

An Amish population has collected among the natives all the way from Madisonburg to Mifflinburg. This is farmland. The Amish businesses are all little shops like the harness shop. In addition many of the women sell produce and eggs from their farmhouses. Simple signs out front will tell you. There are no "see the Amish" commercial attractions of any kind here, nor is it appropriate to stare, ask impudent questions, or try to photograph the Amish people. They don't mind your photographing

Rebersburg Post Office

their farms, barns, and buggies. The people welcome you as a serious customer just as they welcome the local non-Amish population who do business with them. You'll find their English good and their monetary skills excellent.

To clear up another common misconception, although the Amish grow much of what they eat, they generally are not natural-food fans. They drink Kool-Aid, eat Cheerios, make Jell-O, and bake white breads and very sweet pies and cakes. You'll see all this firsthand if you stop in the ◆**Madisonburg Bake Shop** diagonally across the road from the harness shop. The goodies include fresh-baked cakes, pies, including the mandatory shoofly, sticky buns, moon pies, and bread, as well as cider in season, an assortment of handcrafts, and sometimes eggs or produce. The shop is open Monday and Friday 7:00 A.M. to 8:00 P.M.

49

and Thursday and Saturday 7:30 A.M. to 5:00 P.M. It is closed Tuesday, Wednesday, and Sunday.

The bake shop is at the corner of the road. Round the bend and continue following the road to the ❖ **Brush Valley Greenhouse,** where you can find vegetable plants, bedding plants, houseplants, and seasonal gift plants. You're welcome to browse as long as you please; hours are 8:00 A.M. to 5:00 P.M.

The road that runs in front of the greenhouse continues around another curve or two, then brings you back out onto Route 192. As you continue toward Rebersburg, you'll pass several more greenhouse signs that point up long dirt lanes to farmsteads against the mountains or along the creek. The names on these change from time to time, but in this part of the state, it's a fair bet that anywhere a small commercial greenhouse is established it will continue operating under *somebody's* management. Each of these places is unique. If you're in the mood for exploring paths way off the beaten one, drive back a couple of the lanes where you see signs. Drive slowly—the lanes will probably be rough.

In Rebersburg take a few minutes to stop and look at the old homes and churches along the main (and only complete) street. The state's historical society has been actively photographing them to have a permanent record. As local residents become increasingly interested in historic restoration, they're stripping away sidings and interior changes that were added to "modernize" the old buildings.

The ❖ **Rebersburg Post Office** on Route 192 is worth a long look, too. It's housed in a pie-wedge-shaped tan-and-green building that was built specifically as a post office in 1950 and designed by Palmer Bierly, postmaster at the time. Palmer had worked a lot of years in the old post office across the street, a dimly lit little office in one side of the house he lived in. It didn't even have a place at the back of the building to unload the mail. Palmer spent his spare time doodling, eventually coming up with this wedge-shaped building with big glass windows on both sides, glass on the front door, and a roof that is scalloped like the top layer of a fancy wedding cake. The windows were for light; the roof was "just for pretty." Palmer retired in 1970 but his house is still right next door, so he keeps track of what's going on. The two subsequent postmasters have liked the unique appearance and workable interior of the post office and don't mind the people who stop to take pictures. They say Palmer's design helps them in keeping track of all those dozen or so Amish Stoltfus families, some of whose names differ only by a middle initial, as well as about the same number of Bierly families who aren't in the post office business. For all of them it's just part of home. Barbara Brueggebors, writing in the *Centre Daily Times,* offers this view from the outside: "There's something positively heart-warming about the funky little frame building with the protruding glass snout and wedding cake top."

Driving from Rebersburg to Lewisburg takes forty to fifty minutes, longer if you slow down to enjoy the scenery or if you get stuck behind a tractor or buggy for a few miles. The road passes through **Raymond B. Winter State Park,** one of the prettiest parks, with picturesque streams, rhododendron, and especially nice picnic and swimming facilities, all conveniently near the road.

THE UPPER SUSQUEHANNA

Lewisburg is a town oozing history, on the Susquehanna River. It is the home of **Bucknell University,** a historic school. As with most towns, however, the history of the town is in the downtown area, not even hinted at by the entrance, a strip city like those on the outskirts of most old business districts. But even on the strip, you'll find more that is appealing to an off-the-beaten-path traveler than in most such commercial areas. Right where Route 192 joins Route 15, and just about half a block north of where Route 45 joins Route 192, a pleasant, inexpensive place to pick up a good meal is **Bechtel's Dairy and Restaurant,** famous for homemade ice cream but also serving good sandwiches, homemade soups, homemade pies, and salads, as well as heavier dinner entrees. The Bechtel family started the restaurant in 1923. Today a granddaughter manages the restaurant. The friendly, family feeling persists even though the place is large enough to handle lots of customers at once. You'll recognize it by the large model cow on the roof. The restaurant is open Monday through Saturday 7:00 A.M. to 10:00 P.M. and Sunday 11:30 A.M. to 10:00 P.M.

The **Lewisburg Days Inn** is a pleasant place to spend the

night. This is an older motel that has been completely renovated. It is between Routes 45 and 192 on Route 15. The atmosphere here is almost familylike. The atmosphere from the days before renovation and a franchise has not changed in the ways that matter. People working in the area on temporary projects and people waiting to move into permanent homes stay here, as do many regular travelers. Players on softball teams that have games nearby also stay here, but they are not rowdy. Call (717) 523–1171.

Increasingly, this area, with its historic homes, is becoming gentrified. That's good news and bad news. It means the old homes are being restored and preserved. It also means that some of them, as private homes, can only be enjoyed from outside. A map of historic sites for self-guided tours is available from the Visitors Bureau at 219D Hafer Road. Call (717) 524–7234.

One home you can count on getting to see inside is the ◆ **Packwood House Museum,** at 15 North Water Street, right beside the river. It was built in the late 1700s as a tavern and hotel serving travelers along the Susquehanna. They kept enlarging the place, until by 1869 it had twenty-six hotel rooms and a baggage room, reading room, barroom, dining room, kitchen, sitting room, and parlor. According to local history the hotel went out of business in 1887, partly because of the temperance movement. Another owner added on to it, converting it all into townhouses.

And then John and Edith Fetherston, Lewisburg natives, bought it. At this point the story ceases to be an average local house history because the Fetherstons were, well, unusual. She considered herself a painter and a collector. He was an engineer who thought that everything she did was just wonderful. Moreover, he made enough money for her to be able to do as she wished. They renamed the property Packwood House after their estate in England and began filling it with the pieces Mrs. Fetherston collected and the pictures she painted. John died in 1962; Edith followed ten years later, leaving the house and everything in trust to be operated as a public museum.

"The result," as one tour guide put it, "is twenty-seven rooms full of stuff." In the tavern alone, there are 700 items. Mrs. Fetherston apparently collected impulsively and eclectically, buying whatever caught her eye when she traveled. The result is a mixture of fine pieces and near junk that makes touring the house much more fun than visiting museums where you spend all your time in awe. Real people with real personalities come alive at this place. Here a huge Tiffany chandelier is in the same room with a copper brazier that was probably used for cooking in the desert, with a conch shell to blow into to summon servants, with a dentist's chair to—who knows what? Items range from quality reproductions and good antiques to handcrafted regional items. You'll find more glass, china, silver, and crystal in the cupboards than in most gift shops.

Strangely, although Mrs. Fetherston did not have children and is said not to have cared for them, she collected children's furniture, dolls, books, doll furniture, and toys. It's all here. Her paintings are all here, too. One of the reasons John wanted the house to become a museum after he died was so that there would be a place to display her paintings. Among them are surrealistic, pastel flower arrangements, sometimes seeming to float on the canvas because she didn't paint in the horizon line. She painted a series of pictures featuring her white chickens. One, of a rooster in the yard with two hens, is entitled, "The Bridegroom Cometh."

In establishing the museum the trustees put in a glass case behind which you can see exposed parts of the original structure. You can pick up some quality handcrafted items in the museum gift shop. Museum hours are Tuesday through Saturday 10:00 A.M. to 5:00 P.M. and Sunday 1:00 to 5:00 P.M. You can't just wander through here; the house may be visited by tour only. The last tour begins at 4:00 P.M., and the house is closed Mondays and holidays. The admission fee is moderate. Call (717) 524–0323 for information.

Another house to tour, if you like Victoriana, is the **Slifer House Museum,** about a mile north of town on U.S. Route 15. This building dates from 1861. It is considered a good example of Victorian architecture and has been restored nicely. The house overlooks the Susquehanna River. Inside you'll find some interesting Victorian furniture. This museum is unusual in the amount of freedom visitors have; they may even sit in the chairs and play the piano. Guided tours are available April through June by appointment. A modest admission fee is charged. Call (717) 524–2271.

While you are in the area, pick up unusual gifts at ❖ **Colonial Candlecrafters,** a workshop and salesroom where you'll find all kinds of handmade candles, including some that are handpainted and many that are designed for specific special occasions, such as weddings. This place has an odor-eliminator candle that beats anything in an aerosol spray can and a triple-scented jar that makes simple potpourri look tame. You can also buy supplies to make your own candles here: wax, scents, wicking, coloring, and complete candle-making instructions from the knowledgeable people in the shop. On some days you may tour the workshop. Colonial Candlecrafters is on U.S. Route 15, 6½ miles south of I–80 exit 30 South and is open Monday through Thursday, Saturday, and Sunday from 10:00 A.M. to 5:30 P.M. and Friday to 9:00 P.M. The phone number is (717) 524–4556.

ORGANIC FARMLAND

While you're in the Lewisburg area, it's worth taking a side trip to visit ❖ **Walnut Acres** in Penns Creek. For more than forty years, the Keene family has raised and sold grains, beef, and chickens without pesticides or chemical fertilizers on the Walnut Acres farm. Even if you're not particularly interested in such food, the farm is beautiful, the family's accomplishment remarkable, and the guided tour of the little bakery and cannery in the old barn fascinating. The mill and store sell freshly ground, refrigerated flours, all kinds of freshly baked whole-grain breads and cookies, and a broad assortment of beans, nuts, grains, and cereals. The Keene family has won praise from such natural-food specialists as the authors of *Laurel's Kitchen* for producing wholesome food and maintaining a human scale in their successful operation. There are rest rooms, a lunch counter, a wooded picnic area close to Penns Creek, and all the untreated deep-well water you want.

You'll enjoy Walnut Acres more if you know a bit about the Keene family. About fifty years ago Betty and Paul Keene started the project together. She was the daughter of a missionary in India; both she and Paul were teachers. They came to Pennsylvania with a baby and a small child, more or less broke, to live in an old (even then) farmhouse with no bathroom or furnace. The wood-and-coal cookstove heated the house. A single cold-water faucet was the extent of their running water. Generations before the idea caught on, they determined to grow food without using poisons or chemicals on the soil, building the soil instead of simply feeding the plants quick fertilizer fixes. They thought that if they could grow plants sufficiently strong and healthy, in natural conditions, they wouldn't need insecticides because the plants would be naturally resistant to insects and disease. They kept track of how much the soil was improving by how soon the bugs began to leave. Paul recalls that it took them fifteen years to get everything in balance, but it worked. The farm prospered, the Keenes prospered, and the business grew.

Today the Walnut Acres products are still processed by hand, vegetables such as peas are picked without machines, and tomatoes are peeled with knives instead of being dipped in lye. Although their catalogs are now in full color and their order department is computerized, the place still looks and operates like a family farm, with local folks contributing to the labor force. No matter how modern order fulfillment and shipping become, the farming doesn't change. In fifty years no fertilizers or chemicals have been used on the soil. Walk along the edge of a field. The soil is so friable you can almost work it with your hands. The difference is especially striking because commercial farming and canning operations throughout this part of the country have reduced some fields to gullied hardpan that have had to be put out of production and now stand fallow, mainly sprouting thistles.

Betty Keene, who'd lived for years longer than expected with an inherited disease, died recently. She worked in the office until a few days before her death. Some of the Keene children continue with the farm, as does Paul, who writes the catalog copy, including a long essay in each issue about our oneness with nature. The Globe Pequot Press has published a collection of these essays, *Fear Not to Sow Because of the Birds*. It's available through the farm.

If you find you have a taste for the Walnut Acres foods, you can continue eating them when you return home; they ship all over the country. Hours are Monday through Saturday 9:00 A.M. to 5:00 P.M. and Sunday noon to 5:00 P.M. Closed holidays. Call (717) 837–0601. To get there take Route 104 from Mifflinburg south to Penns Creek. Watch for a turnoff sign on the east side of Route 104 at the north end of the village. Walnut Acres is two minutes from that point.

HOME OF LITTLE LEAGUE

If the kids are with you, you might go back to Route 15 in Lewisburg and take the trip of about 30 miles north to Williamsport, home of Little League Baseball, to see the ❖ **Peter J. McGovern Little League Baseball Museum.** In addition to looking at the exhibits of uniforms, safety equipment, and Little League history and changes, the kids can bat and pitch in safety cages and then watch the instant replay on video monitors. In the theater the family can watch documentary films and old World Series games on film. They can test their knowledge on Little League and Major League rules at an electronic quiz board and also see and handle Little League equipment in various stages of production. The museum is open daily, except for Thanksgiving, Christmas, and New Year's Day. Exact hours vary with the season and day. For details about the day you plan to visit, call (717) 326–3607. Admission cost is modest for adults and nominal for children and senior citizens. The museum is on U.S. Route 15, 18 miles north of I–80.

Another interesting stop in Williamsport is the **Lycoming County Historical Museum,** displaying artifacts found locally that trace the stages of Indian culture from 10,000 years ago until the time of the first settlers. Other exhibits include a colonial kitchen, a quilting demonstration, a one-room school, the Indian Diorama of Bull Run Village, and a lumbering diorama. There is a gallery devoted to the history of lumbering in the area and an 1870s Victorian Parlor from "Millionaire Row." **Millionaire Row** in Williamsport dates back to when lumbering was a boom industry in Lycoming County, and Williamsport was the home of more millionaires per capita than any other city in the country. Also in the museum, the **Shempp toy-train collection,** one of the finest toy-train collections in the United States, consists of 337 complete trains and 100 individual locomotives. The trains are American Standard gauge, Early Standard gauge, and O gauge. Hours are Tuesday to Friday 9:30 A.M. to 4:00 P.M., Saturday 11:00 A.M. to 4:00 P.M., and Sunday 1:00 to 4:00 P.M. Closed Sundays and holidays October 31 to May 1. Modest admission. The museum is at 858 West Fourth Street, and the phone number is (717) 326–3326.

If the glimpse of a millionaire's parlor whets your appetite for more, take the Millionaire Row Tours, guided tours or walking tours of a row of mansions on West Fourth Street. Call the Lycoming County Tourist Agency to make arrangements or for more information (717–326–1971).

Then you can actually sit in a Victorian parlor of equal quality by spending the night at ◆ **Reighard House Bed and Breakfast Inn,** a brick and stone Victorian home with six guest rooms, all with private bath. The inn is the family home of Sue and Bill Reighard, who opened the bed-and-breakfast after retirement. The Eastlake furniture in the parlor has been in the family for four generations. No doubt you'll get a glimpse of Sue's humor. She is the kind of person who says, "I'm real good with corn flakes," while she's spreading a full country breakfast in front of you. Her easy good humor and the presence of competent staff make this place a cheery survivor in a business (B&Bs) that produces a lot of burnout. The inn is at 1323 East Third Street, Williamsport (800–326–8335).

For dinner in yet another Victorian mansion, try the **Peter Herdic House,** at 407 West Fourth Street in Williamsport. The house is on the National Register of Historic Places, but, of course, you can't eat that. The menu is Continental, with fillets, chicken, and seafood among the favorites and French pastries for dessert. It is open Monday through Saturday 5:00 P.M. to midnight. Call (717) 322–0165 for information.

WOOL COUNTRY

For people who like to shop in out-of-the-way places, a logical place to go is Woolrich, where you can poke through ◆ **The Woolrich Store.** This is something like the L. L. Bean of Pennsylvania. Woolrich woolen fabrics, ready-to-wear clothing, and outdoor clothing are all for sale here at discount prices. Craftspeople may be interested in the bins of wool scraps for making braided rugs. The store is open Monday through Thursday 9:00 A.M. to 6:00 P.M., Friday and Saturday 9:00 A.M. tp 9:00 P.M., and Sunday noon to 5:00 P.M. The phone number is (717) 769–7401.

On the way to Woolrich, it's fun to take Route 287 north from Route 220, 4 miles to Salladasburg and ◆ **Cohick's Trading Post,** a general store selling groceries, hunting and fishing supplies, and famous homemade ice cream that even Katharine Hepburn has gone out of her way to taste. It is open from 7:00 A.M. to 9:00 P.M. daily; call (717) 398–0311.

Also on the way to Woolrich, it's fun to run through the little town of Hublersburg to get a taste of the kind of place that doesn't dress up for company because they don't expect any. It took the settlers of Hublersburg five tries to settle on a name. The place was first called Logan and was part of Lycoming County in 1829. About ten years later it became part of Centre County, and the name was changed to Hublersburgh. Three years later the name changed again, to Heckla. And three years after that, back to Hublersburgh. The *h* on the end of the name was typical of Pennsylvania spelling for all burghs at the time. Not until May 1893 did Hublersburg settle in with its current name. The official founding date is 1832.

The village is about 8 miles east of Pleasant Gap, on a short spur just south of Route 64. It has a population of a hundred or so people, with names like Dietrich and Heckman. Mostly older people live here. They spend time rolling old newspapers into logs to burn in their fireplaces and keeping track of who has the current honor of being the oldest in the community. Many of the old homes stand pretty much as they've always been, little modernized, certainly not self-consciously restored. It's the kind of drive that begs you to make up stories about the people and places as you pass through.

NORTH CENTRAL PENNSYLVANIA

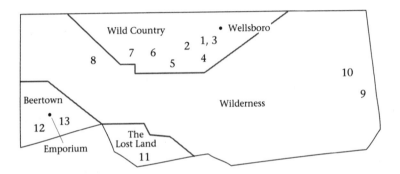

1. Pine Creek Gorge
2. Leonard Harrison State Park
3. Colton Point State Park
4. Penn Wells Hotel
5. The Log Cabin
6. Pennsylvania Lumber
   Museum
7. Susquehannock Trail
8. The Ice Mine
9. World's End State Park
10. Ricketts Glen State Park
11. Frenchville
12. Straub Brewery
13. Bucktail State Park

NORTH CENTRAL PENNSYLVANIA

WILD COUNTRY

A look at the map tells you a lot about the north central part of Pennsylvania. So does the common saying, "You really have to want to be there to get there, but it's worth the trip." From Williamsport Route 15 goes north to Mansfield at Route 6. Or from Route 220, between Williamsport and Jersey Shore, pick up Route 287 north to Wellsboro and Route 6. The area is mountainous and wooded, constituting mostly state parks, wilderness, and some slightly more civilized picnic areas. Unquestionably, the single most notable natural feature in the area is ◆ **Pine Creek Gorge,** more commonly known as the Grand Canyon of Pennsylvania. It is 50 miles long and 1,000 feet deep, covering 300,000 acres of state forest. There are two state parks, ◆ **Leonard Harrison State Park** (717–724–3061) on the east rim and ◆ **Colton Point State Park** (717–724–3061) on the west, from where you can stop at many lookouts and pick up short hiking trails that don't require backpacking or safari gear. Leonard Harrison State Park has a good nature center and a relatively easy trail along the rim to give you an overall orientation to the canyon. More ambitious hikes that take in creeks and waterfalls are possible if you follow Turkey Path about a mile down to Pine Creek. The area is noted for a variety of ferns and songbirds. In Colton Point State Park you can pick up an easy mile-long loop to hike through a hardwood forest rich in astonishingly fragrant mountain laurel with its slightly sticky blooms, where you'll also find wildflowers. Most people visit the Grand Canyon of Pennsylvania in the fall for the foliage, but spring is really a nicer time, especially if you enjoy songbirds and wildflowers and like to avoid other tourists. In winter these are good places for such activities as cross-country skiing and riding snowmobiles. The gorge is 10 miles west of Wellsboro on State Route 660.

To enjoy the area fully, it's a good idea to stop first in Wellsboro to get an area map from the Wellsboro State Chamber of Commerce, P.O. Box 733, 120 Main Street, Wellsboro 16901; (717) 724–1926.

Wellsboro is the Tioga County seat. It's a beautiful little town, with fine old trees and gaslights along the streets in the style of its New England founders from the beginning of the 1880s. You'll find more than a half dozen places to lodge there. The ◆ **Penn Wells Hotel** has a pleasing old-style dining room, the **Penn Wells Dining Room,** that features a Saturday smorgasbord and a Sunday brunch in addition to moderately priced luncheons and dinners. Cocktails are available. Call (717) 724–2111 for hotel and dining room information. About a block and a half away, the **Penn Wells Lodge,** which used to be called a motel, has more modern facilities and now offers an indoor swimming pool, a Jacuzzi, an exercise room, and a sauna. These facilities are available to guests of the hotel as well as those of the lodge. The phone number at the lodge is (717) 724–3463. You can contact the hotel, dining room, or lodge on a toll-free number, (800) 545–2446. For casual dining, ◆ **The Log Cabin,** about 15 miles west on U.S. Route 6, is fun. Here you can eat steaks or seafood in the moderately high price range. Hours are 4:00 to 9:00 P.M., until 10:00 P.M. Friday and Saturday, and Sunday noon to 9:00 P.M. Cocktails are available; call (814) 435–8808.

Also west of Wellsboro, on Route 6 across from Denton Hill State Park at Galeton, the ◆ **Pennsylvania Lumber Museum** depicts the history of Pennsylvania's prosperous lumbering activities a hundred years ago, when the white pine and hemlock in the woods were worth more than gold. The museum displays more than 3,000 artifacts related to the logging business, and the tour includes a walk among the old buildings of the logging camp and sawmill, all surrounded by Appalachian Mountain wilderness that makes the lumbering days feel very much alive. The complex includes Cook Shack, the mess and bunk halls, the sawmill, and a logging pond. The hours the museum is open change from time to time, so it is a good idea to call ahead before you visit. Phone (814) 435–2652. The admission fee is modest.

For hikers the 85-mile ◆ **Susquehannock Trail** can be entered here, as can countless marked trails in the state forests.

WILDERNESS

Farther away, about 50 miles west of Wellsboro, still on Route 6, in the little town of Coudersport, population less than 3,000, you can visit ◆ **The Ice Mine,** a phenomenon of nature where the hotter the weather becomes, the more ice forms, while in the coldest part of winter, there's no ice at all. At Coudersport take Route 44 a few miles north to the mine.

Two other near-wilderness parks that you really have to want to get to, and equally worth the time, are ❖**World's End State Park** and ❖**Ricketts Glen State Park,** in the northern tier of Central Pennsylvania. Part of the fun of World's End is its high elevation and primitive quality. It is not on any major road. Once you leave Route 220, going west on Route 154 will get you there. It's a good place for picnicking, fishing, swimming, and boating. Cabins are available for rental. They are very rustic. You may prefer to stay in one of the boardinghouses or tourist homes in the nearby town of Eagles Mere, where you'll also find a number of simple eating places. The park phone number is (717) 924–3287.

Ricketts Glen is considered by knowledgeable outdoorsmen and women to be the most spectacular of Pennsylvania's state parks. Its more than 13,000 acres of mountains, streams, waterfalls, and lakes spread through Sullivan, Columbia, and Luzerne counties. There are twenty-three named waterfalls, a virgin hemlock forest in which many of the trees are more than 500 years old, a number of trout pools in **Kitchen Creek,** and bass in **Lake Jean.** You'll also find a beach for swimming on this lake. The park has 20 miles of hiking trails, some strictly for the physically fit and some shorter loops that are less strenuous. One trail along the gorge gives you a view of many waterfalls and is breathtakingly close to the edge. Astonishingly, except for locals, relative few people know about the park or visit it. It is possible to find deserted hiking trails almost anytime and wander into the woods feeling like the only person in the forest primeval. Food is available in more cleared areas. Cabins are available for rent and the park has good camping for recreational vehicles (if you don't mind driving one up such steep roads) and tenters. The least arduous way to get there is to take Route 487 from Route 220 at Dushore to Lake Jean. The park phone number is (717) 477–5675.

THE LOST LAND

Going to ❖**Frenchville** can't be an afterthought; you have to make up your mind to make the trip. No place in Pennsylvania could care less about enticing tourists. In fact, as recently as the

1960s, researchers going there preferred to travel in pairs because they expected to be unwelcome to the point of shotgun fire. The little village of several hundred people hides in a pocket of hills in the mountainous area of Clearfield County, near no major city and no important landmark. Your drive takes you through the kind of countryside that science-fiction movie producers look for to film prehistoric earth. The trip over pitted blacktop roads winds through the remains of played-out strip mines, some of them growing scraggly conifers planted as part of reclamation projects. The few outsiders who venture to Frenchville come because of the language. People in Frenchville speak a classically pure French, without any American accent and without the slang of contemporary French streets. Hardly a generation ago most of the adults could not read or write French. Even the inscriptions on tombstones are misspelled and grammatically incorrect. But the people *speak* French flawlessly.

What seems to have happened begins nearly 150 years ago, when the villagers' French ancestors walked overland from parts of Baltimore and New York to settle here. Apparently they walked because when they signed their purchase agreements for what seemed like bargain terms (twelve acres free with each fifty bought), they didn't understand that they were making a deal for isolated land inaccessible by normal transport. In this isolation people farmed, mined, worked on nearby railroads as they developed, and stuck together, speaking French among themselves. Outside the community they spoke a little English, but since nobody got into extended conversations with foreign miners and railroad workers, it didn't add up to much. As new inventions came along, the villagers simply incorporated English words for them into their talk—*automobile, radio, television*. Aside from such words, the language in Frenchville remained pure, classical French.

Consolidated schools educating children outside the community have been diluting the effect for the past ten or twenty years, as has television, but you can hear the old speech still, from villagers named Roussey, Rogeux, Habovick, and Plubell, people who remember apple-butter-making parties and village festivals. The best way to get a taste of the phenomenon and of a special village is to park your car, walk the streets, wander through the graveyard inspecting headstones, stop into the few stores, the tavern, and perhaps the post office, and simply, respectfully, listen. To get to Frenchville go north on Route 879 from I–80 to Clearfield. After your visit to the town, you may want to return to Clearfield, where you'll find fairly inexpensive rates at any one of several good-quality standard motels. You may enjoy walking the Clearfield streets to see several historic buildings that are still in full use downtown.

BEERTOWN

Not near anything else in this northern tier, at an altitude of 1,702 feet, the little city of St. Marys has one major claim to fame in the eyes of Pennsylvanians— ◆ **Straub Brewery,** at 303 Sorg Street. Straub's is one of the smallest independent breweries left in the United States. It produces a beer (made only of water, malt, grains, and hops, with no sugar syrups or additives of any kind) that people who love beer rank above any American and most imported beer. The company distributes only within a radius of 150 miles, which means to get the beer, you either have to be in the area or entice a friend from the area to visit you bearing gifts. *The Connoisseur's Guide to Beer* has named Straub's one of the five best-tasting beers in the country. For people who value the quality, taste, and individuality of a pure beer brewed in a tiny brewery, it's worth a drive to tour the plant and stock up. St. Marys is where Routes 255 and 120 intersect, between Ridgeway and Emporium. Hours are Monday through Friday 9:00 A.M. to noon for free tours and tastings. The brewery is closed holidays. Call (814) 834–2875.

From Emporium the 23,013-acre ◆ **Bucktail State Park** extends down along the Susquehanna River southeast to Lockhaven. State Route 120, a good road between the mountains, makes this a pleasant, scenic drive through some of the wildest country in Pennsylvania, because Bucktail is surrounded by more state forests and parks, wild areas, and natural areas, but if you're in the mood for a more active experience, the place is full of hiking trails and clearings where you can enjoy the view and a picnic. You can count on being alone here. Incidentally, the park's name comes only indirectly from the deer of the same name; the park commemorates a regiment of woodsmen from the area who called themselves the Bucktail Regiment when they served in the Civil War.

SOUTH CENTRAL PENNSYLVANIA

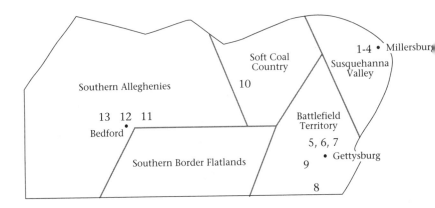

Southern Alleghenies

Soft Coal
Country

10

1-4 • Millersburg

Susquehanna
Valley

13 12 11
Bedford

Battlefield
Territory

5, 6, 7

• Gettysburg

Southern Border Flatlands

9

8

1. Millersburg Ferry
2. Katy's Kitchen and Tea Room
3. Hunters Valley Winery
4. Duncannon
5. Gettysburg National Military
   Park
6. A. Lincoln's Place

7. Eisenhower National Historic Site
8. Historic Fairfield Inn
9. Hickory Bridge Farm
10. East Broad Top Railroad
11. Espy House
12. Old Bedford Village
13. Jean Bonnet Tavern

SOUTH CENTRAL PENNSYLVANIA

SUSQUEHANNA VALLEY

Most people driving along the Susquehanna River between Sunbury and Harrisburg take Routes 11 and 15 on the west side of the river for speed; but on the east side the less-traveled Route 147 gives you some lovely glimpses of the river valley and the tiny, interesting river towns that dot the shores. In Millersburg the ◆**Millersburg Ferry,** the only surviving ferry on the Susquehanna, still runs a mile back and forth at one of the widest points of the Susquehanna, connecting Millersburg with Perry County near Liverpool. A Historic Site Landmark, the first ferry went into operation in 1825, an improvement for passengers and freight haulers over the rowboats and pole boats they'd been using. At the peak of river commerce, four boats made the trips. Now only the Falcon and Roaring Bull, heated by woodstoves in winter, remain, and it's a pretty casual operation. A rough sign lettered on four boards nailed horizontally to a post says: FERRY IS RUNNING/DRIVE DOWN THE HILL/AND I'LL COME/AND GET YOU. You sort of have to guess when, knowing that the trip, one way, takes about twenty minutes. Each ferryboat accommodates four cars and sixty passengers. Without your car you could almost wade the mile; the river at this crossing rarely goes more than 3 feet deep. To find the pick-up point, drive into Millersburg on Route 147 and follow signs to the crossing site. Generally, the ferry runs spring, summer, and fall. Exact dates vary with the weather and the economy. Call the ferryboat office at (717) 692–2442 for more information.

While you're in Millersburg wander through the historic section to see the old buildings, then run over to 107 Market Street for a bite to eat in ◆**Katy's Kitchen and Tea Room.** The restaurant building used to be the Auchmuty House, built by Samuel Auchmuty in about 1868 and inhabited by his eccentric daughters, Annie and Eugenie, who stuffed the upstairs back rooms to the ceiling with isinglass containers and kept money under the floorboards in the bedroom. The isinglass containers are gone, and no doubt the money is, too, but the rooms downstairs are still quaint, if not eccentric, with all kinds of handmade country collectibles (which are for sale) crammed on the shelves of antique cupboards. The tearoom is known for its cranapple tea and an assortment of soups, salads, and sandwiches and mud pie for dessert. It is open Tuesday through Saturday 11:00 A.M. to 2:00 P.M.; call (717) 692–4543.

Whether you cross on the ferry or drive south to the bridge at Clarks Ferry, eventually you'll want to get to the other side to explore **Perry County.** At Liverpool, just off Routes 11 and 15, across from the ferry landing, ◆ **Hunters Valley Winery,** on a 150-year-old farm in the valley, combines traditional winemaking methods with such new technology as stainless steel fermenters and fine filtration to produce wines. Its grapes come from vineyards planted on the high slopes overlooking the Susquehanna River in 1982. In many ways the growing conditions resemble those in parts of France, with full sun, good air circulation, excellent water drainage, and temperatures moderated by the river and mountains. Visitors may walk through the vineyards and picnic on the grounds. Open Thursday 11:00 A.M. to 5:00 P.M., Friday 11:00 A.M. to 7:00 P.M., Saturday 11:00 A.M. to 5:00 P.M., and Sunday 1:00 to 5:00 P.M. Call (717) 444–7211.

South of Liverpool, still on Routes 11 and 15, drive through ◆ **Duncannon,** a little railroad and river town featured a few years ago in *National Geographic* for its continuing sense of working-class neighborhood rather than for being picturesque. In Duncannon, people still borrow a cup of sugar, bring food when someone in the family dies, and talk about what's happening at church. Because of its proximity to the Appalachian Trail, it's become a rest spot for hikers, who usually stay at the old Hotel Doyle, on Market Square. You'll find several eating places, including a diner, in and around Duncannon. Stop at least for coffee to give yourself a chance to listen to the local talk.

Elsewhere in Perry County you could drive for a couple of days, through about 550 square miles, trying to take in all the historic and natural attractions—fourteen covered bridges, twenty-four old mills, twenty-seven historical locations, fourteen hiking trails, ten scenic overlooks, three national natural landmarks, six rural parks, and a partridgeberry tree. Write for a booklet listing and showing locations of all the attractions as well as hotels and eating places: Perry Tourist Bureau, Box 447, New Bloomfield 17068 (717–834–4912). Ask for their literature even if you can't go there.

These people formed a volunteer tourist bureau producing booklets and brochures worthy of special mention. They'll tell you that in 1980, one of their Holstein herds produced the highest milk and butterfat ratings in the state on a per-cow basis; their chickens laid an average of 262 eggs per bird, and their cornfields yielded sixty bushels of corn per acre, all for total production running up to eight digits. They print older folks' recollections of a father who raced the train on his bicycle while the passengers cheered, laundry baskets and washtubs full of food hauled to annual picnics, and fiddlers who picked up the tempo to keep dancers hopping. Also, they sell appealing prints of historic landmarks in Perry County done by local artist Scotty Brown. The prints have appeared in the publicity and history brochures. What an antidote to airbrushed color photos emblazoned with screaming headlines and printed on fifty-pound glossy paper! Pure Pennsylvania.

BATTLEFIELD TERRITORY

You shouldn't miss Gettysburg, where the Yankee and Confederate soldiers fought the bloodiest battle of the Civil War in 1863. Admittedly, the area is slickly organized for tourism, but the history is well and interestingly communicated, and the area feels more rural than urban. ◆ **Gettysburg National Military Park** surrounds the city of Gettysburg. The visitor center (phone 717–334–1124) is across from the entrance on State Route 134. Battlefield tours start from here, and exhibits explain the battle. The most dramatic exhibit, in Cyclorama Center, complete with a sound-and-light show, centers around Paul Philippoteaux's famous 1884 painting, *Pickett's Charge*. Elsewhere in the center, displays of Civil War weapons and uniforms complete the picture. Because the battlefield is 6 miles by 7 miles, you may want to take a bus tour with the Gettysburg Tour Center. A stereo narration re-creates the Battle of Gettysburg as the double-decker bus crosses the battlefield. The tour takes about two hours. The center (717–334–6296) provides free shuttle service to and from all major motels and campgrounds.

At least two dozen attractions related to the Battle of Gettysburg and the Civil War clamor for your attention, including **The National Civil War Wax Museum** (717–334–6245), the **Jen-**

Hall of Presidents

nie Wade House and Olde Town (717–334–4100), and **Gettysburg Battle Theatre** (717–334–6100). **The Hall of Presidents** features wax reproductions of thirty-six presidents that, with the help of light and sound, tell "The Story of America" in their own voices. For a complete listing of attractions, dining, camping, and lodging, write Gettysburg Convention and Visitor Bureau, 35 Carlisle Street, Gettysburg 17325, or call (717) 334–6274.

In one form or another, try to catch a live performance of James A. Getty as Abraham Lincoln. For more than a decade, Getty and his wife, Joanne, have run ◆ **A. Lincoln's Place,** a multifaceted business centered around his forty-minute performances as Lincoln. The shows trace Lincoln's life from his boyhood in Kentucky through his presidency. The Gettys came from Illinois, naturally knowing a little something about Lincoln, but

James was a choral conductor, neither an actor nor a historian. Then he grew a beard and, Mrs. Getty says, "The beard made him do it." Getty immersed himself in research about Abraham Lincoln and then began his performances. "Now we know a *lot* about Lincoln," Joanne Getty says. James tailors his shows to the age level of his audience, changing them as his continuing research turns up new information. He performed at both the A. Lincoln Place Theatre in Gettysburg, where Mrs. Getty managed the theater and its gift shop, and on tour. James's shows won the Pennsylvania Travel Excellence Award. The theater has closed because James and Joanne couldn't keep up the pace any longer and because he'd become too busy to maintain his research. But the touring performances will continue, as will local performances at **The Conflict Theatre,** 213 Steinwehr Avenue (717–334–8003). At the time of this writing, Getty's performances are scheduled for 8:00 P.M. Monday through Friday in the summer, but these hours and possibly even the location could change. He almost certainly will perform at other places and times in Gettysburg, probably several times a day, as ever. The telephone for A. Lincoln's Place will ring, as it always has, in the Gettys' home (717–334–6049). Call to learn where you can see a show before you visit the area. A performance by a man whose beard led him to study and portray Lincoln and whose passion makes him keep a business phone at home embodies the very spirit of this book.

Also at Gettysburg, the ❸**Eisenhower National Historic Site** recalls and commemorates Ike's military and presidential years. The easiest way to get there is on a shuttle bus from the **National Park Visitor Center.** The site, open to the public, includes the Eisenhower 230-acre farm and farmhouse, the only home the Eisenhowers ever owned; a putting green and sandtrap once given to the president by the Professional Golfer's Association; and a brick barbecue grill where Ike broiled 3-inch-thick steaks for guests. Eisenhower's shooting range, cattle barn, and the milk house where the Secret Service office was ensconced are not open to the public yet. The home was not opened to the public until 1980, shortly after Mamie died. Visitors find the farmhouse homey rather than grand, not really decorated, but rather simply furnished almost entirely with gifts showered on the Eisenhowers during his forty-five years of national service. On the glassed-in porch where the couple preferred to spend their time stands an unfinished painting by Ike. He completed at least 260 others during the last twenty years of his life. A few of them hang in the house.

Eisenhower said he could get a better sense of what a person was truly about by entertaining him at home. Guests included Nikita Khrushchev, Charles de Gaulle, and Winston Churchill. Visiting here brings the presidency and world figures into an uncommonly human focus. There is a modest admission charge. The hours and the number of visitors allowed vary—call first (717-334-1124).

To dine and bed down in the spirit of Gettysburg's history and Eisenhower's farm, there are two places to consider: ◆ **Historic Fairfield Inn** or ◆ **Hickory Bridge Farm,** both only about ten or twenty minutes from the battlefield. At the Historic Fairfield Inn, in the village of Fairfield, you stay in one of two guest rooms, with shared bath, in the plantation home of Squire William Miller, who laid out the town in 1801. The building became an inn in 1823. Country cooking is the big attraction here—crab cakes or chicken and biscuits, lots of vegetables, and homemade fruit cobblers with ice cream. The inn and restaurant close from time to time for holidays and vacations. Make plans and reservations well ahead of time. Call (717) 642–5410. Hickory Bridge Inn, in Ortanna, run by Nancy Jean Hammett and Mary Lynn Martin, offers seven rooms, including cottages, with private bath. It's a genuine farmstead with a red barn-turned-restaurant, a country museum with old farm equipment, a pond, and a trout stream, surrounded by fifty acres of farmland. Literature about the place claims that guests swim in the spring-fed pond in summer, but anyone who's ever stuck a foot into spring water at the source will take that information skeptically. The rooms are quiet, furnished with Pennsylvania Dutch items and antiques, and the cottages have wood-burning stoves. In the restaurant you're offered amazing quantities of Pennsylvania Dutch cooking in a designer-country setting, Friday and Saturday nights and Sunday noon to 3:00 P.M. The inn is closed from just before Christmas until the first of the new year. Call (717) 642–5261 for more information.

At 44 York Street, the **Brafferton Inn,** the first home in the original historic district, is a 1786 stone building furnished with colonial antiques. Full breakfast is served. Phone (717) 337–3423.

For a complete list of operating bed-and-breakfasts, write the Gettysburg Convention and Visitor Bureau, 35 Carlisle Street, Gettysburg 17325, or call (717) 334–6274.

SOUTHERN BORDER FLATLANDS

More Civil War history waits at Chambersburg, the next major stop on Route 30 west after Gettysburg. In the 1960s Chambersburg won recognition, along with several other smaller Pennsylvania cities, for early efforts to preserve historic areas as part of city development plans. While the city could claim much history, actual historic buildings were in such short supply that saving them seemed especially important because the Confederates occupied the city three times during the Civil War. The last time, in 1864, 3,000 Confederate soldiers rode into town demanding $100,000 ransom in gold. Chambersburg couldn't pay; the Confederates burned the town, putting two-thirds of its citizenry out of homes. Then the raiders rode off to McConnellsburg. Mention it the next time someone talks about Sherman burning Atlanta. Pick up a brochure with a mapped walking tour of downtown Chambersburg at the chamber of commerce, 75 South Second Street.

This is a pleasant, interesting area. In addition to walking through Chambersburg, you might like to stop at the **Cumberland Valley Visitor Station** at exit 6 off I–81 (1235 Lincoln Way East) to pick up brochures for a driving tour of the town and for other towns in the area. The center has a picnic area and nature walk. Call (717) 264–7101.

SOFT COAL COUNTRY

Head on toward McConnellsburg, on the heels of the Rebel warriors, to pick up Route 522 north, crossing the Pennsylvania Turnpike and continuing north to the ◆ **East Broad Top Railroad,** a Registered National Historic Landmark at Orbisonia. Some railroad buffs will certainly argue that East Broad Top is the best train attraction in Pennsylvania. It is the last 3-foot-gauge (narrow-gauge) line in the east still operating from its original site. It was built in 1873 to move coal from the bituminous coal mines of Central Pennsylvania to Mt. Union, where the coal was dumped into standard-gauge cars on the Pennsylvania Railroad. The EBT hauled coal until 1956! Today the train runs a 10-mile trip that takes almost an hour, hauling mostly nuts—the people kind, not the tree kind. Not only does the EBT attract railroad enthusiasts, it also calls to photographers and sound-recording nuts. Crazy guys with absolutely top-quality recording equipment show up every so often, lugging Nagra tape recorders and stringing microphones all along the track to record the Doppler effect or to try to get the chuggs and choos of the train's coming and going recorded in stereo to pick up background sounds for a film or media show.

For just plain folks the ride is scenic, fun, and educational. In the roundhouse you can still look over several steam locomotives and puzzle over the M-1 gas electric car built in the mid-1920s with help from Westinghouse at EBT shops. Complete picnic facilities are available at the end of the line. Often folks stop there and come back on a later train. All up and down the line, you can either be a nut or watch the nuts. It's a plain good

East Broad Top Railroad

time. Trains leave once an hour from 11:15 A.M. to 3:30 P.M., weekends only, June through October. Rates are moderate. Write EBT Railroad, Rockhill Furnace 17249, or call (814) 447–3011.

SOUTHERN ALLEGHENIES

Going to Orbisonia will have taken you off Route 30. At this point you can either head to the center of the state on Routes 22 and 322 to arrive in State College or to drive east to Harrisburg, or you can backtrack briefly on either the Pennsylvania Turnpike (not recommended) or Route 30 to Bedford and Bedford Springs in the Allegheny Mountain area. Settlement here goes back to 1751. Much of the area's history is preserved in restored and reconstructed buildings. In the historic district start at the visitor information center at 141 South Juliana Street in Bedford. It's open Monday through Friday 9:00 A.M. to 5:00 P.M. and Saturday 10:00 A.M. to 2:00 P.M. For more information call (814) 623–1771 or (800) 765–3331. Pick up a map and information for a self-guided tour that will include at least thirteen sites. One of these, ◆ **Espy House,** dating back to the late 1700s, served as the headquarters of George Washington when 13,000 troops came here to put down the rebellion of citizens in the "Whiskey Belt" against an excise tax on whiskey—the 1794 Whiskey Rebellion.

At another stop you can still see the trenches by the road where in 1863 troops dug in against Confederate soldiers expected to attack the railroad at Altoona. The rebels marched toward Gettysburg instead, making the trenches unnecessary. President James Buchanan came to take the healing waters at Bedford Springs and made the springs his Summer White House.

◆ **Old Bedford Village** re-creates Pennsylvania pioneer life, with more than forty log homes and craft shops, one-room schools, and other buildings brought from different places and rebuilt here, reproducing a colonial village. More interesting than the buildings, costumed guides and artisans demonstrate an unusually large variety of early skills and crafts—potting, making brooms, cooking, weaving baskets, tanning hides, even firing long rifles. The activities sprawl over seventy-two acres, though of course not all the land is used for buildings. But it's a lot of walking; the tour takes three hours. Old Bedford Village accommodates people in wheelchairs. Sometimes a tour of this length tempts kids to try to hitch a ride; sometimes gracious people let them. Old Bedford Village is open daily to the public except for a period from the end of October to mid-January. Old Bedford Village schedules an almost continuous string of special festivals and demonstrations. Write for further information to P.O. Box 1976, Bedford 15222, or call (814) 623–1156 or (800) 238–4347. Moderate admission is charged.

At the ◆**Jean Bonnet Tavern,** one of the oldest taverns in Western Pennsylvania (circa 1762), 4 miles west of Bedford on Route 30, try a steak dinner, the tavern's specialty. The dining room and tavern areas are separate and are open daily beginning at 11:00 A.M. Call (814) 623–2250.

If you keep going west on Route 30, **Coral Caverns,** 7 miles from Bedford, offers tours of the only known coral reef caverns, formed more than 300 million years ago while the area was still covered by the Appalachian Sea. Open June weekends 10:00 A.M. to 5:00 P.M., daily July 4 through Labor Day 10:00 A.M. to 5:00 P.M., and September weekends 10:00 A.M. to 5:00 P.M. Halloween festivities are held in October on Friday and Saturday nights from dark until 10:00 P.M. Admission prices are moderate. Call (814) 623–6882 for details.

NORTHEASTERN PENNSYLVANIA

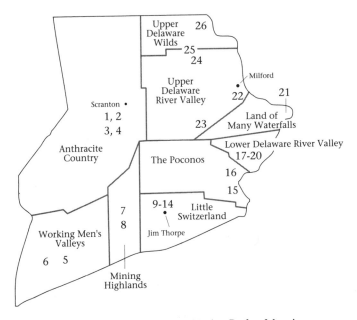

1. Scranton Iron Furnaces
2. Steamtown Historic Site
3. Pennsylvania Anthracite Museum
4. McDade Park
5. Pioneer Tunnel Coal Mine
6. Anthracite Museum at Ashland
7. Beacon Diner
8. Nesquahoning
9. The Jim Thorpe Mausoleum
10. Jim Thorpe Railroad Station
11. Old Mauch Chunk Scale Model Railroad HO Display
12. Cat's Paw Gallery
13. St. Mark's Episcopal Church
14. Asa Packer Mansion
15. Cherry Valley Vineyards
16. Quiet Valley Living Historical Farm
17. Delaware Water Gap
18. Mary Stolz Doll and Toy Museum
19. The Pocono Indian Museum
20. The Pennsylvania Crafts Gallery
21. Bushkill Falls
22. Cliff Park Inn
23. Sterling Inn
24. Settler's Inn
25. Roebling Inn on the Delaware
26. Sylvania Tree Farm

NORTHEASTERN PENNSYLVANIA

ANTHRACITE COUNTRY

To understand eastern Pennsylvania, you need to understand coal mining. The anthracite coal region of eastern Pennsylvania is not particularly pretty. Although some stretches of highway through the hills are lovely, much of the landscape has been marred by the coal-mining operations that used to be the economic mainstay of the region. Nor can the working mines be called aesthetically pleasing by any usual standard. But the area is historically rich, not with battle sites or great government buildings but in the details that let us see how people there used to live and work. Nowhere is it more obvious than in Scranton, where coal and iron were at their peak until the end of World War II, when the demand for coal diminished. In downtown Scranton, on Cedar Avenue, between Lackawanna Avenue and Moosic Street, the ◆**Scranton Iron Furnaces** are open daily from 8:00 A.M. to dusk. These four huge blast furnace stacks, built between 1841 and 1857, are the remnants of the iron industry around which Scranton grew, with coal mining and railroads falling into place as companion industries. Admission is free; call (717) 963–3208.

Emphasizing the relationship between iron, railroads, and coal, within walking distance of the iron furnaces, is a terminal at Lackawanna Station for the ◆**Steamtown Historic Site,** a working steam railroad on which you can take a scenic ride from Scranton to Moscow, about 12 miles south, and back. Schedules vary so call for information. The development in process includes a visitor center and a museum complex at the original roundhouse. The actual site is open daily from 9:00 A.M. to 6:00 P.M. from the end of May until late October. For more details about train schedules and fares, call (717) 340–5200.

Continue your education by going through the ◆**Pennsylvania Anthracite Museum,** which features exhibits related to the lives and work of the ethnic communities in the region. Exhibits survey activities related to canals, railroads, silk mills, and factories, and, of course, coal. The museum is on Bald Mountain Road in Dade Park. Take the North Scranton Expressway to the

Keyser Avenue exit. Follow Keyser Avenue and the signs to McDade Park. The museum is open 9:00 A.M. to 5:00 P.M. Monday through Saturday and from noon to 5:00 P.M. Sunday. Admission is modest. Closed on major holidays. Call (717) 963–4804.

◆ **McDade Park** has picnic tables and charcoal burners if you'd like to snatch a bite before going on to the Lackawanna Coal Mine Tour, which begins next to the museum. This tour takes you down into an actual abandoned slope mine to see what the miners did and what conditions were like there. Tourists are lowered from the loading platform to the mine interior in an electrically hoisted car. The big yellow iron car and hoist are new and were designed especially for this purpose, so you need not worry that you'll be in an old creaking car of the sort you've seen in old movies. Inside the mine a tour guide, either a retired miner or a teacher who's been trained by a retired miner, will take you on a 600-foot walking tour on a wooden walkway, explaining what you see and answering questions. The underground area is spacious; even claustrophobic visitors shouldn't feel closed in. Mannequins in mining clothes and a life-sized stuffed mule add verisimilitude. Although the mine isn't really dirty, it is underground, and coal can leave its marks, so consider this a blue-jeans-and-walking-shoes excursion. The tours last about an hour. New tours leave hourly, more frequently during busy times. More exhibits and artifacts are housed above ground in a new addition to the building called **Shifting Shanty.** From May through October, tours begin at 10:00 A.M.; the last tour leaves at 4:00 P.M. Moderate admission is charged. Call (717) 963–6463.

WORKING MEN'S VALLEYS

From Scranton you can get to Hazleton quickly on I–81, or cross over to Route 11 and drive down along the Susquehanna for a while to see some of the little river towns. These are not the picturesque, renovated towns of slick decorating magazines, but real, working towns inhabited by Pennsylvania's laboring folks. Driving through here you may still see women wearing babushkas (head scarves), kids scuffing their shoes on the sidewalks, and town merchants sitting in front of their stores during idle moments. From about Wilkes Barre, the drive becomes especially mountainous in the narrow river valley, giving you the sensation that the mountains are close around your ears. Almost any time you tire of it, you can pick up a short road back to the interstate to Hazleton, another coal town that has now moved into other kinds of industry to compensate for the spent mines and the declining demand for coal. Here, **Eckley Miners' Village** gives you a chance to visit a spot that is part historic site and part living community. It is authentic, not because it has been re-created, but because it never has changed. How could one re-create the black silt heaps and open strip mines and slag left from earlier operations surrounding the village? It was a company town from its settlement in 1854 until 1971. Now it's administered by the Pennsylvania Historical and Museum Commission, but more than fifty people—retired miners, their widows, and children—still live here. The village, covering one hundred acres, includes fifty-eight buildings and exhibits showing what daily life was like for coal-mining families. These people were the ethnic groups of immigrants who found their work in the coal fields: first English, Welsh, and Germans, then Irish and Eastern Europeans. The village is 9 miles east of Hazleton, off State Route 940. Follow signs to the site, which is open Monday through Saturday from 9:00 A.M. to 5:00 P.M. and from noon to 5:00 P.M. on Sunday. It is closed holidays, except Memorial Day, July 4, and Labor Day. A modest admission fee is charged. Call (717) 636–2070.

Another interesting pair of stops in the vicinity is the Anthracite Museum at Ashland and Pioneer Tunnel Coal Mine, on State Route 61. Ashland is off I–81 about 20 miles south of Hazleton. ❖**Pioneer Tunnel Coal Mine** is the first mine to have been opened to the public and has been operated as a nonprofit community project for more than twenty-five years. It is a drift mine tunnelled almost horizontally a half-mile into Mahanoy Mountain about 450 feet down. Pioneer Tunnel follows an anthracite vein that is nearly 200 feet thick in some places. The miners who worked in it, before it was blasted shut to close it down in 1931, were able to work standing up. In mines with thinner seams, miners had to work on their knees. The tour, in a small train pulled by a locomotive powered by batteries, begins at the entrance of the mine and passes the big vein, where you can see the tunnels branching off the main tunnel. It takes about a half hour. To see an open pit mine that was dug close to the surface with steam shovels, and a "bootleg hole" where poachers dug out coal, take the steam engine **Lokie** for its half-hour tour around Mahanoy Mountain—on the outside, not through tunnels. To get to Pioneer Tunnel Coal Mine, take Route 61 into Ashland, where it becomes Center Street. Turn left (south) on Nineteenth Street and continue for 3 blocks. The mine is open from Memorial Day to Labor Day 10:00 A.M. to 6:00 P.M. daily, weekends only from Labor Day to October 31. A moderate admission fee is charged. Call (717) 875–3850 for more information.

One street over, the ◆**Anthracite Museum at Ashland** on Eighteenth Street features a collection of tools, machinery, and photographs showing how hard coal has been mined from the early pick-and-shovel days to contemporary surface mining operations. The museum is open from Memorial Day to Labor Day, 10:00 A.M. to 6:00 P.M. Monday through Saturday and noon to 6:00 P.M. Sunday. The rest of the year hours are 9:00 A.M. to 5:00 P.M. Tuesday through Saturday and noon to 5:00 P.M. Sunday. Admission is modest. Call (717) 875–4708.

MINING HIGHLANDS

If you're looking for an authentic view of Northeastern Pennsylvania, not embellished by brochure prose or photographs, try this slightly circuitous drive from Hazleton to historic Jim Thorpe to get a sense of (and participate in) the real day-to-day workings of the area. Take Route 309 from Hazleton south toward Tamaqua. You'll drive through mountain sections that alternately astonish you with their beauty and dismay you with the way that the beauty is marred by the accoutrements of producing, shipping, and using coal—silt, slag, smokestacks, tipples, trucks, and tracks, all seeming anomalies in the landscape, but inevitable in the process. Here and there a tree will grow defiantly out on the slag. In a few miles, at the intersection of Route 309 and Route 54, stop at the ◆**Beacon Diner,** a real old-time diner, silver on the outside, with swivel seats at the counter and booths along the windows. You can order from standard menu choices of sandwiches, specials, fries, and the like, but a better treat is a big, fat, round sticky bun with good coffee or a milkshake made in an honest-to-goodness milkshake mixer from real ice cream and milk. If you sit at the counter, you can joke with the waitresses about whether sticky buns are allowed by Weight

Watchers and eavesdrop a bit to pick up current local small talk.

After refreshment take Route 54 east through ◆ **Nesquahoning,** a little mining town built on hills so steep that nothing seems level. Businesses and homes share the same streets. Driving slowly, you can peek through a barbershop window to glimpse an elderly gentleman getting a haircut while he chats with cronies. In front of the homes, flourishing flowers spill from their beds over cement walls toward the sidewalk. Occasionally a dog threatens a shrub and scampers away when he's reprimanded with a rolled newspaper. In backyards women in jeans or cotton housedresses hang laundry to dry on clotheslines. Then you're through town, and signs lead you down the mountain into Jim Thorpe.

LITTLE SWITZERLAND

If anybody had told the old-timers that one day Mauch Chunk (pronounced *maw-chunk*) would be named Jim Thorpe in honor of an American Indian Olympic athlete and football player from Oklahoma, who was buried here even though he'd never lived here, they'd have smiled. If anybody had said that Mauch Chunk would become a tourist attraction and that the best-selling books in town would be about restoring Victorian homes, the old-timers would have guffawed. Until about 1950, Mauch Chunk was another Pennsylvania mining town whose economy fluctuated with the coal market, where miners lived in uncertainty, and millionaires lived in mansions. Trying to survive, citizens of Mauch Chunk and East Mauch Chunk were donating a nickel a week to an economic development fund. Meanwhile, Jim Thorpe's wife was looking for a way to right a series of insults that had been heaped upon her husband before he died. In 1912 he had won two gold medals and broken many pentathlon and decathlon records to become a hero at the Olympic Games in Stockholm. But when the Olympic Committee discovered that he had played one season of professional baseball for $60 a month, they stripped him of all his awards because he was not an amateur. After he died of cancer, penniless, Oklahoma refused to build him a monument, so his wife started looking for a place where he could be buried with honor. Admiring the fighting spirit of Mauch Chunk and East Mauch Chunk, she approached the two towns with her idea. The towns incorporated to become Jim Thorpe and erected a large granite mausoleum on the east side of town. On the tombstone read the words of King Gustav of Sweden when he presented the Olympic medals to Thorpe in 1912: "Sir, you are the greatest athlete in the world." The monument was never turned into a honky-tonk tourist attraction, but the publicity that came to the town as a result of the change combined with the cooperation between what had been two rival communities helped turn the economy here around. In a posthumous reversal, Thorpe's amateur status was reinstated in 1982. A year later the committee presented replicas of his gold medals to his family. ◈ **The Jim Thorpe Mausoleum** is ½ mile east of Jim Thorpe on Route 903.

Another interesting site, this one overlooking Route 209 at the base of Mount Pisgah, is a memorial plaque where the village of **Northern Liberties** used to be. In 1861 virtually all the village men and boys between the ages of 16 and 26 volunteered to serve the Union in the Civil War, effectively destroying the village by killing off its reproductive population. All that remains is the plaque memorializing the soldiers, attached to a large rock where the village used to stand.

More lighthearted history awaits in the heart of downtown Jim Thorpe. After you drive down the mountain into town, park in one of the public lots or at one of the meters where you still get a hour for a dime to explore the narrow, winding streets on foot. This area at the foot of the hills is Hazard Square. It quickly becomes obvious how it got its name. Drive defensively and walk across the street as if you were in a war zone. At the center of all this, in the ◈ **Jim Thorpe Railroad Station,** you can buy tickets for rides on steam locomotive trains through the mountains to Nesquahoning and back, an 8-mile round trip, in the spring and summer. During the autumn foliage season, longer trips of nearly three hours to Haucks and back leave twice a day. Tickets for the short trip are under $5.00, for the longer trip about $12.00. For complete schedules and rates at the time you plan to visit, write Rail Tours, Inc., P.O. Box 285, Jim Thorpe 18229, or call (717) 325–4606.

Across the street from the station, you see the ◈ **Old Mauch Chunk Scale Model Railroad HO Display** on the second floor of the Hooven Mercantile Company. This spectacular train-lover's display has thirteen different model trains that pull cars over more than a thousand feet of track. The hours the display is open vary seasonally. It's a good idea to call ahead. A modest admission fee is charged. On the first floor of the mercantile building, specialty shops laid out in emporium fashion, without partitions, feature coal jewelry and sculptures, dolls, decorated eggs, and various other craft items and supplies. Call (717) 325–2248 for more details.

One block south of Broadway, Race Street, a narrow alley, winds along the path once taken by an old mill race past old buildings and more specialty shops and Stone Row, built by Asa Packer in 1848. Today longtime residents and shopkeepers live side by side with newly arrived artists and writers. If you are or if you know a cat lover, the ❖ **Cat's Paw Gallery** (717–325–4041) will be a sure stop. It contains a collection of crafts and fine art in ceramic, metal, wood, and glass as well as prints, paintings, and drawings, all inspired by cats and created by well-known artists.

This shop continues to grow in sophistication and in the quality of artists and craftspeople whose work it sells. This is a gallery of fine art and designer-quality studio craft work. You won't find imports or syndicated cartoon figures here. John and Louise Herbster, proprietors, have been developing this gallery since 1985. It goes beyond the sentimentality typical of some theme gift shops. For a long time Louise threatened to get a big neon cat as a sign and, in a sense, she did. A light sculpture that is, in fact, a neon cat, attracts your attention in the window.

A suggestion from Louise about another don't-miss spot is ❖ **St. Mark's Episcopal Church,** also on Race Street. The church is considered one of the most notable of the late Gothic Revival churches in Pennsylvania. It was built in 1835 by Richard Upjohn, a well-known architect of religious construction in his time. He is the same architect who was responsible for the third Trinity Church of New York City.

St. Mark's in Jim Thorpe is laid out in the form of a cross, with an altar of white Italian marble, Minton tile floors, and Tiffany windows. The reredos, of Caen stone, is a memorial to Asa Packer, who was a local magnate of considerable importance. Visitors are welcome in the church. Tours are available summer through October daily. Call (717) 325–2241 for more information.

After having seen the memorial to Packer in the church and

also the stone houses he built, you may want to drive up the hill on U.S. Route 209 to tour the ◆ **Asa Packer Mansion,** providing a dramatic contrast to the cabins of Eckley Miner's Village at Hazleton. The lavishly decorated Victorian home was built in 1850 by European craftsmen and furnished in mid-nineteenth-century opulence. It stands the same today as it was when the Packers celebrated their fiftieth wedding anniversary—preserved rather than restored. Among the outstanding pieces in the house are the first-prize gas chandelier of the 1876 Centennial Exposition and the crystal chandelier copied for the film *Gone with the Wind.* Along with fine carved walnut furniture and the desk, chair, and bookcase belonging to General Robert E. Lee, you'll find good collections of paintings, sculpture, crystal, and china. Asa Packer is said to have earned all this, working his way from humble beginnings to become the founder and president of Lehigh Valley Railroad, founder of Lehigh University, and a philanthropist on the grand scale. Hours of operation fluctuate with the season. Call (717) 325–3229 for details. A modest admission fee is charged.

One of Asa's gifts, possibly philanthropic, to his son, Harry, was a brick and stone mansion in the style of the Second Empire, practically next door. This house is lavish, too, with hand-decorated ceilings and Victorian antiques, including some pieces that belonged to the Harry Packer family. The **Harry Packer Mansion** is open for tours and also operates as a bed-and-breakfast inn, with thirteen rooms, some with private bath, available for guests. A stay includes full breakfast in the morning. The mansion is open for tours Sunday through Friday, noon to 5:00 P.M. The mansion has mystery weekends and also sometimes turns over the entire establishment to wedding parties and special celebrations, so be sure to call before you plan a tour or if you want to spend the night (717–325–8566).

THE POCONOS

Sometimes you see promotional material saying that Jim Thorpe is in the foothills of the Poconos. In Jim Thorpe they like to advertise themselves as the "Little Switzerland of America." As you climb back up the mountains to leave the town, you see where a town looking for tourists got the idea. Unfortunately for those seeking areas yet unexploited, many parts of the rest of the Poconos already have more tourists than they can fit comfortably into heart-shaped bathtubs and serve with fruity pink cocktails at poolside bars. To see some of the lesser known parts of the Poconos, take Route 209 out of Jim Thorpe toward Lehighton. In its time Route 209 was a major highway in the state, important enough to displace homes and cemeteries and prize stands of sugar maples in its construction. This route has lost much tourist traffic to interstates; here and there you still see a failed group of tourist cabins predating today's motels or an abandoned gas station with weeds growing through the macadam. These properties might be good investments for people who can afford to wait for a return, because traveling on I–80 has become nearly intolerable here. Huge repair projects and slow trucks hauling double trailers up the mountains often back traffic up for miles. The highway is in such bad condition physically that it's hard to see how the state will ever catch up. One can imagine traffic returning to Route 209 in sheer desperation. By today's standards it's narrow and slow because of the steep hills and curves, but the surface is in fairly good condition, trucks pull over to let traffic pass, and most of the countryside is lovely. Even where it's not beautiful, it's interesting. This highway skirts Lehighton.

In Lehighton most folks speak in noticeable Pennsylvania Dutch accents; many have lived here all their lives, as have their parents and grandparents and even great-grandparents.

Continue north on Route 209, then take Route 33 south at the Saylorsburg exit. Almost immediately, turn left on Old Route 115, Lower Cherry Valley Road, and follow the signs into the ◆ **Cherry Valley Vineyards,** a friendly little winery run by Dominick Sorrenti and his family. The setting is entirely rural and the atmosphere in the sales room casual. Nobody puts on airs here, even though some of the wines are good enough to warrant it. The Sorrentis have produced a limited amount of absolutely wonderful Chardonnay that they themselves dare to describe as "dry, delicate, incredibly wonderful balance." Well, false modesty serves no one. They also produce a genuinely dry champagne and, for those with sweeter tastes, several fruity semi-dry wines that manage a fresh taste of grapes without being foxey or syrupy sweet. Tours include information about the wine's fermentation, filtering, and bottling processes. The winery is open daily from 11:00 A.M. to 5:00 P.M.; tours are given Saturday from 11:00 A.M. to 5:00 P.M. and Sunday from noon to 5:00 P.M. Call (717) 992–2255.

A quick jog back on Route 33 north takes you to Snydersville, which isn't much more than a gas station and a school bus stop, but several antique dealers have opened shops in old homes here. The names and proprietors may change, but this remains a good area for antiquing, where the dealers are knowledgeable but not in the thick of the tourist stream.

At Snydersville you pick up Business 209 (paralleling Route 209) going toward Stroudsburg. The business route is slower but less heavily traveled and more interesting. Before you get to Stroudsburg, take the Shafer Schoolhouse exit and follow the signs to ◆ **Quiet Valley Living Historical Farm.** The quality of this site and the passion of the people who make it work defy superlatives. More than twenty-five years ago, Alice and Wendell Wicks, with their daughter and son-in-law, Sue and Gary Oiler, saw the possibilities for this Pennsylvania German farm, which dates from 1765. The Wicks and the Oilers poured work and time and money into the project. Researching, repairing, and collecting furnishings and farm equipment, they opened Quiet Valley as a living museum, showing how the original Pennsylvania Dutch family lived on this virtually self-sufficient homestead from 1765 to 1913. For a time the Oilers actually lived in the top floor of the home. Over the following quarter century, with hens and newly hatched chicks at their feet, and sheep, pigs, and other barnyard animals with their young living on the farm, the two families restored the existing buildings to full function and reconstructed others that would have been there.

Using costumed area residents as role players, Quiet Valley takes you through the daily routines and seasonal activities of the colonial family. One of the most interesting parts of the tour is the earthen-floored cellar kitchen in the main building. At first the settling family lived entirely in this room, with only the clay-hearth fireplace for heat and cooking. A costumed guide uses the cooking utensils and talks about her life as a colonial woman. Outside the baker offers you samples of applesauce cake or corn bread from the brick oven. Your kids join kids in costume petting the animals and jumping in the hay. Everybody gets a little dirty, a little itchy, and a little sneezy. Quiet Valley differs from most living museums in the uncanny sense of reality it achieves. It's nice to hold on to the feeling for a while after the tour by picnicking in the grove. Quiet Valley is open June 20 to Labor Day, 9:30 A.M. to 5:30 P.M. weekdays and 1:00 to 5:30 P.M. Sunday. The last tour begins at 4:00 P.M. A moderate admission fee is charged. Call (717) 992–6161.

Should Quiet Valley set you up for more country life, you might drive to East Stroudsburg and spend the night at **The Inn at Meadowbrook,** built in 1842. The inn has sixteen guest rooms, some with private bath. In a country setting of hills and meadows, Meadowbrook offers opportunities for skating, skiing, cross-country skiing, horseback riding, fishing, swimming, tennis, walking, and reading by the fire, depending on your mood and the season. The inn serves dinner for guests as well as the public. The dining room can accommodate up to about forty people. The food includes fresh shrimp, lamb, filet of beef, and a special concoction of chicken and shrimp sautéed in champagne. For full details write the Overmans, R.D.7, Box 7651, East Stroudsburg 18301, or call (717) 629–0296.

LOWER DELAWARE RIVER VALLEY

From here you are close to the ◆ **Delaware Water Gap.** It is part of a National Recreation Area between New Jersey and the Pocono Plateau in Pennsylvania. Publicity calls it "the eighth wonder of the world." Even in the nineteenth century it attracted the well-to-do for resort holidays away from the heat. The beauty of the gap lies partly in the contrasting colors of layers of quartzite, red sandstone, and dark shale that have been revealed as the river eroded its path even deeper over geologic eons. One way to see some of this, yet get a break from driving, is to ride the **Delaware Water Gap Trolley.** Like most development around the Water Gap, the tour is frankly commercial. Guides give a spiel about history, points of interest, settlers, and Indians, but it would be a shame to miss the natural splendor of the gap chewed through the mountains by the Delaware River because of a superficial and not necessarily permanent layer of commercialism. The trolley depot is on Route 611 at the center of Delaware Water Gap.

With a little light hiking, you can appreciate the gap closer at hand. Park in the Resort Point parking lot off Route 611, on the Pennsylvania side. Across the road stone steps take you to a trail paralleling a stream that goes up steeply for a short distance, then turns left onto a marked trail. The trail continues gently upward for about a mile, and when you get to a waterfall, you can no longer hear the traffic on Route 611. A little farther straight ahead, a large rock outcropping overlooks the entire gap. In this area you can also drive into some overlook points from which you see a spectacular view without hiking. Signs direct you to these. At one such place a souped-up red Chevrolet once roared in, a couple of teenagers slurping diet Cokes looked out, said, "There isn't anything here," and roared away. It happens regularly. Pushing these people over the edge is against state and national regulations. For full information on the Delaware Water Gap National Recreation Area, write to the offices, Bushkill 18324 or call (717) 588–6637.

In the same area, off Route 209 at Bushkill, the ◆**Mary Stolz Doll and Toy Museum** features about 125 dolls representing cultures from around the world, as well as many miniature rooms Mary has created and an assortment of related old toys. The collection began when Mary started collecting dolls in 1910. Her interest has been continued in the family for four generations. Bill and Jan Stolz own the museum now. Looking without touching in such places isn't too difficult; looking without owning can be sheer torture for a committed collector. The gift shop offers relief in its collection of dolls, teddy bears, doll houses, trains, and miniatures. The museum is open seven days a week; call for hours (717–588–7566).

Directly across from the doll museum, ◆**The Pocono Indian Museum** shows the history of the now-extinct Delaware Indians in six rooms of collected artifacts. Visitors listen to a half-hour tour cassette explaining the displays as they walk through the exhibits. Some of the pottery is more than 1,000 years old. Weapons and tools have had only their handles reconstructed. The Delaware Indians didn't fit the stereotype typified by the drugstore wooden Indian. They wore simple deerskin garments, cut their hair short, and used no feathers, except perhaps a few for ceremonies. Nor did they live in tepees. One room in the museum holds a reconstructed bark house of the kind the Delawares made for themselves by lashing together saplings and covering them with strips of elm or oak bark. Another room in the museum exhibits artifacts from various western Indian tribes, even a 130-year-old scalp. If that seems a little gory, you can cover your eyes as you pass. In the museum gift shop, you can buy souvenirs made by surviving Indian groups. Hours are daily, 9:00 A.M. to 7:00 P.M. in the summer, 9:30 A.M. to 5:30 P.M. beginning in September. A modest admission fee is charged. Call (717) 588–9338.

Also on Route 209 at Bushkill, ◆ **The Pennsylvania Crafts Gallery** exhibits and sells the work of juried members of the Pennsylvania Guild of Craftsmen: weaving, pottery, gold, silver, brass, pewter, soft sculpture, leather, Scherenschnitte, basketry, and so on. It is open year-round 11:00 A.M. to 5:00 P.M.; closed Tuesday and Wednesday. Call (717) 588–9156.

LAND OF MANY WATERFALLS

Even more glorious than the creations of any human hand, ◆ **Bushkill Falls,** known as "The Niagara of Pennsylvania," is easy to reach, 2 miles northwest of U.S. Route 209. Easy walking over rustic bridges and a nature trail of about a mile and a half takes you through virgin forests, past a gorge from where you can view eight waterfalls, the largest of which is Bushkill, dropping 100 feet. These falls have attracted generations of artists and photographers. Even with a simple camera it's possible to take spectacular pictures. You may picnic, boat, and fish in the park. Some food is available. The park is open daily 9:00 A.M. to dusk April through November. Rates are moderate. Call (717) 588–6682.

At Dingmans Ferry, farther north on Route 209 but still in the Delaware Water Gap National Recreational Area, **Dingmans Falls,** the highest waterfall in Pennsylvania, pours down over 100 feet of rock with awesome power. On the same easy trail, in woods of hemlock and ferns, **Silver Thread Falls,** not quite as high but equally beautiful, is another stop worth a few photographs. In the park's nature center, you can study an audiovisual program or pick up a map and talk to a naturalist about the falls and good trails to walk. You'll find lots of easy trails here, good for those whose fitness falls short of perfection.

Delaware Water Gap

UPPER DELAWARE RIVER VALLEY

From Dingmans Ferry it's only about 10 miles more to Milford, a good place to spend the night—or several nights if you can spare the time. A good choice is the ❖ **Cliff Park Inn,** completely surrounded by a golf course that has been in operation since 1913. Talk about a mature course! This inn, an 1820 Buchanan farmhouse, has three dining rooms serving food one guest called "a gourmet's dream." She was hooked by the quail stuffed with raisins and apples, flamed in brandy, and covered with a truffle sauce. Since the menu changes from time to time, you may find not quail but some other exotic offering, such as a game pie or beef Wellington. In winter, when even the fanatics don't try to

91

golf in Pennsylvania, the golf course is used for cross-country ski-ing. The nearby hiking trails that are so nice in summer also make great ski trails when there's snow. If you're a learner rather than a pro, the notion that golf courses don't have rocks to dent you when you fall should please you, as should 600 acres of woods and a view that overlooks three states merging onto the Delaware River. You can rent all the equipment you need right at the inn. In addition to ten rooms with private bath, the inn rents three cottages. Write the inn at Milford 18337, or call (717) 296–6491 or (800) 25–6535.

While you're in Milford, stop at the **Upper Mill,** a nineteenth-century water-powered mill where water rushing over a three-story-high waterwheel powers the grinding stones and generates enough electricity to light the mill. The mill is open from May to Thanksgiving 9:00 A.M. to 5:00 P.M. daily, with frequent tours and demonstrations. Call for fall and winter schedules. The mill (717–296–5141) is on Sawkill Creek and Water and Mill streets.

From Milford, driving west on I–84 for about half an hour brings you to another place it would be pleasant to spend several days, the ◆**Sterling Inn,** in South Sterling. It's a fifty-four-room hostelry on more than a hundred acres, with hiking and cross-country ski trails, a nine-hole putting course, a tennis court, and a swimming and skating pond. Twelve of the rooms have fireplaces or Franklin stoves. Trained chefs produce American country gourmet food, including beef, chicken, seafood, such veal dishes as osso buco, and fruit and berry pies. Saturday-night entertainment is live jazz or contemporary music. Write Sterling Inn at Box 2, South Sterling 18460, or call (717) 676–3311 or (800) 523–8200 for rates and reservations.

For a different kind of stay, go northwest from Milford on Route 6 to try ◆**Settler's Inn,** run by Grant and Jeanne Genzlinger. This twenty-room family-style place, furnished in "early attic" and run with lots of help from family and friends, is casual in everything except food, which is definitely full-scale gourmet—baked stuffed shrimp, broiled lamb chops, veal Oscar, pecan torte with strawberry filling—all the foods that you should pat directly on your hips, since that's where they end up anyway. The inn is near Lake Wallenpaupack, where you can fish and boat. For more information about Settler's Inn, write 4 Main Avenue, Hawley 18428, or call (717) 226–2993.

UPPER DELAWARE WILDS

The Lackawaxen area deserves some of your attention, even if you don't get into the rustication of the tree farm. The area is only a couple of hours away from New York City, yet it remains unspoiled because the stretch of Delaware River from just north of Port Jervis to Hancock, New York, is protected under the Wild and Scenic Rivers Act of Congress. You'll find most of the historic and natural attractions along or near Route 590. The village of Lackawaxen is named for the river that flows into the Delaware. *Lackawaxen* is the Indian word for "swift waters." If you're a fishing enthusiast, you'll like the Lackawaxen Fishing and Boat Access, which gets you to a notably good fishing area where the Delaware River runs deep and slow.

For landlubber history, the **Zane Grey Home** right across from the fishing access represents a kind of classic American success story. By profession Zane Grey had been a dentist and a semiprofessional baseball player. Perhaps he got tired of trying to keep his baseball cap separate from the caps he put on people's teeth, or perhaps he got tired of being berated in baseball and being feared in the office. At any rate, in 1905 he gave up molars and mounds and turned to writing westerns. He said the Lackawaxen area was where he first became familiar with "really wild country."

His books were so convincing that Hollywood took to them, and by 1918 Zane had left for California to work with the people producing movies based on his books. His Lackawaxen home remains as a museum containing mementos of his life. He and his wife got back to the wilds, in a sense. They are buried in the cemetery of St. Mark's Lutheran Church (built in 1848) along with the body of an unknown soldier from the Revolutionary War killed during the Battle of Minisink in 1779.

From the fishing access you can also see the **Roebling Aqueduct,** engineered by the same man responsible for the Brooklyn Bridge, John Roebling. The aqueduct, originally shaped like a deep trough to serve as a channel for barges between Delaware and Lackawaxen River sections of the canal, was built in 1848–49 for the D & H Canal Company and is remarkable in that, unlike many structures on the Delaware, it has remained sturdy enough to be in use, almost a century and a half later, as an automobile bridge. It is the oldest suspension bridge in use today.

A nice place to stay, where the owner is deeply engrossed in local history, is the ◆ **Roebling Inn on the Delaware**. It's on Scenic Drive off Route 590 at Lackawaxen. JoAnn Jahn says the white clapboard inn with green shutters and a green roof was built about 1870 and was used in earlier years, back when the canal was in operation, as an office for the D & H Canal Company. The guest rooms here are decorated with country antiques and modified for contemporary tastes with private baths, television, and queen-sized beds. From here you can walk to everything—canoeing, golf, horseback riding, a bait shop, a lunch restaurant, a general store, white-water rafting, tennis, river swimming, and a couple of great places for dinner. This is a real treat if your idea of a good time is being free of your car for a while. For full details and reservations write P.O. Box 31, Lackawaxen 18435, or call (717) 685–7900.

A considerably more rustic alternative to Sterling and Settler's is a country vacation at ◆ **Sylvania Tree Farm** on the Delaware River in Mast Hope. Mast Hope is one of those you-can't-get-there-from-here places. From Milford take Route 6 about 14 miles to Route 434, go north about 3 miles to Route 590 west to Lackawaxen, then turn right toward Mast Hope. Ask for a brochure with full directions when you make your reservations. The destination worth the trouble of all these little roads is 1,250 acres on the river shore with woods, fields, brooks, and seclusion. You can stay in a modern cottage or pitch your tent at a campsite. It's a naturalist's paradise. The property is in the Upper Delaware Wild and Scenic River corridor, administered by the National Park Service. Watchful visitors sight bald eagles and blue heron in the valley and white-tail deer, black bears, beavers, and foxes in the woods and fields. You can cross-country ski in winter, hike other times, and book canoe and rafting trips with nearby outfitters. Also, the National Park Service gives tours of the river valley and several historic sites. Write Sylvania Tree Farm, Box 18, Mast Hope, Lackawaxen 18435, or call (717) 685–7001. Visit here secure in the knowledge that you'll never hear those dread words made famous by social directors in the more glitzy Pocono resorts: *Everybody down to the lake for a weenie roast!*

Southeastern Pennsylvania

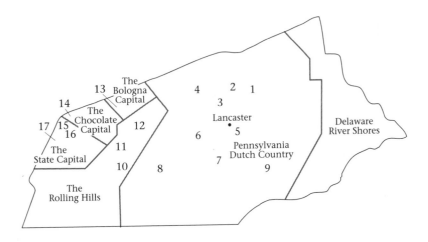

The Bologna Capital
13

14

The Chocolate Capital
17 15 16

12

The State Capital

11

10   8

The Rolling Hills

4   2   1

3

Lancaster
5

6

Pennsylvania Dutch Country
7   9

Delaware River Shores

1. Daniel Boone Homestead
2. Antique Airplane Restaurant
3. Shillington Farmers Market
4. Conrad Weiser Homestead
5. The General Sutter Inn
6. Sturgis Pretzel House
7. Candy Americana Museum
8. Watch and Clock Museum
9. Railroad Museum of Pennsylvania
10. Mt. Hope Estate and Winery
11. The Cameron Estate Inn
12. Cornwall Iron Furnace
13. Weaver's Famous Lebanon Bologna
14. Hershey's Chocolate World
15. State Museum of Pennsylvania
16. Museum of Scientific Discovery
17. Boiling Springs

Southeastern Pennsylvania

Pennsylvania Dutch Country

In this part of Pennsylvania, paths have been not only beaten but also flailed, paved, and planted with billboards. Unquestionably, the main attraction has been Pennsylvania's "Plain People"—the Amish. The "Fancy" Pennsylvania Dutch of hex signs, *schnitz und kneep*, scrapple, and shoofly pull a close second. The official center of tourist activity—Lancaster and the little towns nearby with racy names like Intercourse, Blue Ball, and Bird-in-Hand—does not appear in this guide because the area is nearly touristed to death. Although more than 16,000 Amish still live here, a steady emigration to escape tourism and to find more farmland for the children in their large families has spread the Amish population through virtually all of Pennsylvania's rural areas. Almost any of them offer an off-the-beaten-path traveler a less frenetic, more tasteful opportunity to learn about the beliefs and customs of the Plain People, or at least of the Amish. Moravians, Mennonites, and Dunkards, also historically part of Pennsylvania's tradition, have escaped the commercial blitz.

As for the Fancy Dutch, those lovers of art and color and music, commercialization makes it hard to sort out the authentic from the bogus. There are just too many cute sayings, too much "home cooking," too many placemats and T-shirts printed with stylized tulips and birds.

The character of the area has changed not only because of tourism but also from increasing population. Rural villages swelled into Reading suburbs. One-room schools in Shingleton, Fleetwood, and Breezey Corner, where kids named Yenser, Schmidt, Dietrick, and Schucker used to leave their shoes outside the schoolhouse doors after they'd been sprayed by skunks caught in their trap lines, now house corporate executives. Expensive shrubs replace the old outhouses. A swimming-pool company takes over the abandoned post-office building. In place of the worn old realities, recreations and specialty shops scream for tourist dollars.

The burgeoning factory-outlet business has also changed the character of the area. Literally hundreds of outlets, mostly housed

Daniel Boone Homestead

in old factory complexes in Reading, attract shoppers by the busload. Sometimes they stay for a week or longer to work through the outlets looking for bargain prices on brand-name merchandise. Motels and restaurants geared to the bargain-hunting family increase in number yearly. Whatever the value of the phenomenon to the local economy, it dilutes the local, homey feel of the area and fills up spots that until recently were still hideaways.

But don't yield to the temptation to skip the whole thing and head for uninhabited hills, because at the fringes of official Dutch country, you can still find towns where people go about their work much as ever, cook and serve the hearty meat-and-potatoes stuff of their ancestors, and speak about everyday things, without scripted sayings, in the quick cadences of inherited German accents. So chust you vait oncet before you give up. There's good here yet, say not?

Start 9 miles east of Reading on Route 422 at the ◆ **Daniel Boone Homestead.** Judging from the number of Boonetowns, Boonevilles, and Boones in the country, ole Dan'l got around, leaving historic sites wherever he stopped. He was born at this homestead to frontier parents in 1730 and raised here among the few English Quaker, German, Swiss, Huguenot, and Swedish pioneers who settled the area. He lived here for sixteen years, raising cattle for his father and getting friendly with the Shawnees, who probably taught him many of the outdoor skills he used the rest of his life. The restoration of the Boone Homestead, which was done mostly between 1940 and 1950, includes the foundation of the original log house and an addition the Boones built of stones, as well as a barn, blacksmith shop, and sawmill. The furniture is not what the Boones had, but the antiques all date from the 1780s and were gathered from the area. Guided tours lasting about forty-five minutes show how the Boones lived and also explain the differing practices of the various other cultures represented in Pennsylvania in the 1700s. The guides go into considerable detail about the history and uses of the furnishings as well. In addition to the buildings, the homestead has 600 acres of fields, woods, and a lake. Walking and biking trails are open from dawn to dusk daily. The area abounds in songbirds, wildflowers, and wildlife, including painted turtles that sun themselves on rocks protruding above the surface of the lake. With a little more exploring you can discover a woodchuck den, parts of a chestnut fence, and trails left by small animals. The homestead is open Tuesday through Saturday 9:00 A.M. to 5:00 P.M. and Sunday noon to 5:00 P.M. It is closed Monday and holidays, except Memorial Day, July 4, and Labor Day. There is a modest fee for touring historic buildings. Call (610) 582–4900 for more information.

To get back to those human needs that can't be satisfied by history and hiking, if you'd like a novel place to eat where the food is basically Pennsylvania Dutch without being self-conscious about it, stop at Dutch Colony Motor Inn and ◆ **Antique Airplane Restaurant** at the East Junction Reading Bypass and Route 422 (4653 Perkiomen Avenue) east of Reading. Suspended from the ceiling, a Monocoupe built in 1927 in Illinois could still fly today if you took it outside and gassed it up. Breity Breithaupt, an aviator for forty years, found the plane in a barn in Maine, restored it, and flew it to many antique airplane shows before hanging it from the ceiling of the restaurant he and his wife own. Apparently, the suspension is perfectly safe; the plane has hung there since 1967. Breity has since collected many other

Antique Airplane Restaurant

aviation antiques and artifacts, all of which are displayed on a second-floor balcony overlooking the restaurant. Large photographs of Charles Lindbergh add another touch of early flight nostalgia. The best thing that could happen while you're eating here is that at least one little kid will scamper into the dining room, look up, stand stock still in wonder, and then start dancing about under the plane, pointing up and marveling aloud. The waitresses enjoy it and sometimes even create reasons for children from the motel lobby to go into the dining room. The association between airplanes and bad food doesn't hold here. The food is good; the soups and bread are homemade. People who live in the vicinity eat here and chat with waitresses they've obviously known a long time. Although tourists stop at this busy place too, it feels like family. Should you decide to spend the night, the rooms are large and attractive, with good, quiet central heat and air. A heated swimming pool surrounded by a generous lawn helps you unwind. Rates are moderate; call (610) 779–2345 or (800) 828–2830.

From here a quick jaunt on Route 724 takes you to Birdsboro, a little town that still runs on steel, iron, paper, and textiles and hasn't a hint of anything designed especially for tourists, except perhaps the crude, hand-lettered sign: BIRDSBORO, ESTABLISHED 1740 POPULATION 3,481. Stay on Route 724 as it runs along the railroad tracks about 10 miles to Shillington, where you'll come directly to the ◆**Shillington Farmers Market** at the corner of Lancaster Avenue and Museum Road. This is a place to hear Pennsylvania Dutch rural accents and see produce and baked goods that haven't been hauled long distance in supermarket trucks. In addition to the produce and baked goods, the farmers market sells meats and poultry, all from Berks County, and is open Thursday and Friday 6:00 A.M. to 6:00 P.M. Call (610) 777–0798.

After you eat and shop, take Museum Road back to Route 422 west, heading toward Womelsdorf and the ◆**Conrad Weiser Homestead,** a National Historic Landmark. Conrad Weiser was a colonist who maintained close contacts with the Indians, respecting especially their search for a higher power or Great Spirit and their belief in law built on basic moral values in their families. Perhaps because the Indians appreciated that his understanding differed from the more common view of them as uneducated savages without real culture, Weiser became Pennsylvania's foremost Indian negotiator. He made treaties with the Indians and worked as an interpreter and peacemaker during the French and Indian War. His small stone home, a spring house, and his grave stand on what was once frontier in a twenty-six-acre park equipped with lovely picnic areas and public rest rooms. The homestead is open Wednesday through Saturday 9:00 A.M. to 5:00 P.M. and noon to 5:00 P.M. Sunday; it is closed holidays except for Memorial Day, July 4, and Labor Day. A modest admission fee is charged (610–589–2934).

As long as you're this far south, get on Route 501 and head to Lititz. In the center of town, ◆**The General Sutter Inn,** run by Joan and Richard Vetter, has eleven guest rooms and two suites, all with private bath, and a dining room where the menu dares to deviate from standard Pennsylvania Dutch fare to offer delicacies such as an *escalope* of veal sautéed with wine and mushrooms or chicken Dijon with onions. The inn is named for John Augustus Sutter, who threw himself headlong into the gold rush and never got any of the gold. He came to Lititz to recoup

PENNSYLVANIA DUTCH COUNTRY

and regroup. Moravians built the inn in 1764 and forbade dancing, singing bawdy songs, or cursing inside. It's probably still not
a good idea. John Vetter is a minister, and he has a church organ
in the lobby. Somebody must think of doing a little dancing,
however; the inn has a bar with Saturday-night entertainment.
Joan furnished the inn's rooms with Victorian beds and dressers
and small antique objects. It is open all year except for Christmas
Eve, Christmas Day, and New Year's Day; call (717) 626–2115 for
details and reservations.

While you're in Lititz be sure to visit ◆**Sturgis Pretzel
House** at 219 East Main Street, the oldest pretzel bakery in America. It's hard to explain what pretzels mean to a Pennsylvania
Dutchman, except to say that they don't make them right anywhere outside the state. Julius Sturgis started baking pretzels in
1861 in a bakery that dates back to 1784. This company's got
the hang of it by now. The pretzels are soft, puffy, golden
brown, and salted just enough. Connoisseurs like them with
mustard. Bakers twist them by hand, which isn't as easy as it
looks, as you'll learn when you take advantage of the opportunity to handle a hunk of dough and try it yourself. While
you're at the bakery, you'll see the whole pretzel-making
process—from getting the notion to bake some to the final
cooling. The tour, which takes about twenty-five minutes,
begins with a history of the pretzel, moves to the do-it-yourself
stage, then takes you to the modern machines used for manufacturing hard pretzels. Sturgis still makes all its soft pretzels by
hand, as it did in the 1800s, and bakes them in the original
bakery oven. The last tour begins at 4:30 P.M. Hours are Monday through Saturday 9:00 A.M. to 5:00 P.M., closed January 1,
Easter, Thanksgiving, and Christmas. A modest admission fee is
charged. Call (717) 626–4354.

Also in Lititz, you might stop at the Wilbur Chocolate Company's ◆**Candy Americana Museum** and Factory Candy
Outlet, at 48 North Broad Street. The tour is an entertaining history of American candy making with demonstrations, including
chocolate dipping, and displays of antique equipment. You can
buy candy at discount prices in an outlet that looks like a country
store. Hours are Monday through Saturday 10:00 A.M. to 5:00
P.M., closed Thanksgiving and Christmas. Call (717) 626–1131
for more information.

From Litiz you're a quick hop back toward Lancaster, the area where the Amish first captured the attention of tourists in Pennsylvania. If you're trying for attractions not in the usual tourist stream, you probably won't stop in Lancaster at all, though the beautifully manicured farm properties are lovely to see as you drive by. However, two towns in particular offer glimpses into entirely different worlds. In no particular order, drive into **Strasburg,** a little town with a population of fewer than 3,000, and **Columbia,** a larger town with a population of about 10,000.

U.S. Highway 30 west goes directly to Columbia, home of the ◆ **Watch and Clock Museum of the National Association of Watch and Clock Collectors, Inc.,** which began in a private home and has expanded to attract visitors, collectors, and students from all over the world. The motto of the watch and clock collectors is *Tempus vitam regit,* translated "time rules life." In this museum you'll find about 8,000 items, including clocks, watches, and tools, all demonstrating the importance of time in our lives. The study of time is known as "horology." The exhibits in the museum give you an idea how we've been keeping time over time. The timepieces range from an ancient Egyptian pot that measured dripping water to Stephen D. Engle's "Monumental Apostolic Clock," designed around the actions of the apostles of Jesus. This piece alone, the most popular exhibit, is remarkable enough to make the museum memorable. The clock, in an elaborately carved case, measures 9 feet by 11 feet and contains forty-eight moving figures and eight separate movements. In addition to telling time, the clock shows movement of the planets and plays an organ. After working on the clock for twenty years, Engle finished it in 1877. Then it was lost for a while. It was discovered in upstate New York and acquired in 1986 by the National Association of Watch and Clock Collectors, whose members restored it for display in the museum in 1989.

Other displays include a large collection of grandfather clocks, collections of tower clocks, banjo clocks (considered the first truly American designed clocks), and every sort of pocket watch possible, along with the tools necessary to work on all these timepieces. More old clocks are mounted on the outside of the building and on a tower next to it. In addition to actually seeing the timepieces, you'll pick up some surprising information about them, the kind of thing you'd never think about but grasp immediately as making sense once you hear it. For example, typical clock movements required a lot of brass that came from England. After the Revolution such raw materials were in short supply and American clock designers began experimenting with clocks requiring less raw material. They're on display in this museum. And grandfather clocks were called "tall case" clocks until after the song, "My Grandfather's Clock," became popular.

Not all visitors to the museum are tourists; some people come to take classes in repairing clocks and watches. A staff member observes that digital and quartz timepieces made such repair work seem obsolete for a while but is a growing trade again. The museum is at 514 Poplar Street, off U.S. Highway 30 and State Route 441, corner of Fifth and Poplar streets. It is in an easily seen modern brick building and is well marked with signs. The museum is open 9:00 A.M. to 4:00 P.M. Tuesday through Saturday and noon to 4:00 P.M. Sunday May through September. During the winter months it is closed Sundays. Call (717) 684-8261. Admission is $3.00 for adults, $2.50 for senior citizens, and $1.00 for children ages 6 to 17.

Southeast of Lancaster, at the intersection of State Route 896 and U.S. Highway 30, the town of Strasburg has a replicated Amish village and lots of Pennsylvania Dutch food and atmosphere, but its more remarkable attractions are the railroad museum, the train ride, and a toy train museum—the perfect combination for children and for adult train buffs—especially when you remember that railroads have played an important part in the economic development of Pennsylvania.

The ◆ **Railroad Museum of Pennsylvania,** a state museum, has displays covering rail history from the 1800s to the present, including everything from restored nineteenth-century wood-burning steam engines to diesel and electric locomotives, displayed with appropriate passenger and freight cars at a re-created railroad station. The museum is on State Route 741 east, about a mile from town. It is open Monday through Saturday 9:00 A.M. to 5:00 P.M. and Sunday noon to 5:00 P.M. May through October. During the winter months it is closed Mondays, Veterans Day, Thanksgiving Day, and Christmas Day. Admission for adults is $6.00, senior citizens $5.00, children 6 to 17 $4.00. Call (919) 687–8628.

Right across the road, **Strasburg Rail Road Co.,** a private enterprise, takes about 350,000 people a year on forty-five-minute train rides through Amish country on the oldest short line in the country. The company has four antique coal-burning locomotives and beautifully restored passenger cars. During the peak season, July and August, fourteen rides leave the station daily. After school starts, things calm down a bit. The people who work here manage to communicate enthusiasm for trains and their customers in spite of the big numbers, so don't avoid the place just because it's popular. The Strasburg Rail Road Co. is open daily in the summer, reduced hours in winter. The schedule is complicated so call for current hours; (717) 687-7522. The fare is $7.00 for adults, $4.00 for children ages 3 to 11.

After the riding experience, go about half a mile farther east on State Route 741, then about a block north on Paradise Lane to get to the **Toy Train Museum,** the museum of the National Toy Train Association. Here five separate layouts in five different gauges fill one large room. There are both antique and modern toy trains and a videotape about them. This is your stop if you love old Lionels and the like and want to learn more about them.

Finally, for pure fun, try **Choo Choo Barn, Traintown, U.S.A.,** also on State Route 741. This is the project of enthusiasts —an "oh, wow!" kind of place. As a local resident explained, "A nutty man who loved trains started it and it kept growing, then his nutty sons took it over and it grew some more." In a huge shedlike building you find about 1,700 square feet of miniature displays depicting Lancaster County. There are fourteen operating toy trains and well over a hundred other moving figures and vehicles, as well as scale reproductions of well-known spots in the area. Choo Choo Barn is open every day 10:00 A.M. to 4:30 P.M. from June to the day before Labor Day. It closes an hour earlier the rest of the time; also closed Thanksgiving and Christmas days. Admission is $4.00 for adults, $2.00 children ages 5 to 12. Call (717) 687–7911.

Strasburg has two interesting places to stay—**Historic Strasburg Inn,** One Historic Drive, a full-service 101-room Williamsburg-style inn, and **Strasburg Village Inn,** 1 West Main Street, an 11-room Williamsburg-style bed-and-breakfast inn. Historic Strasburg Inn is an appealing old brick building with gold trim, appropriately furnished with period reproductions and a surprising number of authentic antiques as well, thanks to the efforts of a manager who likes to go antiquing. The inn serves three meals a day, breakfast and lunch being somewhat regional in nature and dinner featuring fine dining. Rates range from the low $60s to about $100, depending on the season, with the lowest rates in the winter. Call (717) 687-7691. Strasburg Village Inn is an elegant two-story house from the late 1700s, also furnished in Williamsburg style. Breakfast is served at the Creamery next door. Rates range from the mid-$50s to about $100, with the lowest rates in the winter. Call (717) 687–0900.

If you are interested enough in old structures to stay in one, you also should spend a little time driving or walking around the area to enjoy the old homes—from modest to magnificent—in the historical community.

THE ROLLING HILLS

From Lititz, take Route 772 west a bit more than 5 miles to Manheim and ❖**Mt. Hope Estate and Winery** for tipple and turrets. The Victorian mansion caters to tourists, but in an unusual and tasteful way, worth your time for a change of pace. A wealthy ironmaster originally owned the mansion, and he systematically surrounded himself with more and more splendor, from hand-painted 18-foot ceilings to imported crystal chandeliers. Today hostesses costumed in clothing from various periods of the family's reign from the 1800s to the Roaring Twenties lead you through the refurbished rooms, explain what life was like here, and then, in the billiard room, offer you tastings from the Mt. Hope wine cellars. If you like any of the wines, you can buy them in the Vintage Wine Shoppe. After the tour you're free to walk about the estate gardens, filled with shrubs and plant specimens from all over the world. The French hybrid grapes from which Mt. Hope wines are made also grow on mansion grounds. It is open Monday through Saturday 10:00 A.M. to 6:00 P.M. and Sunday noon to 6:00 P.M.; closed an hour earlier in winter and on New Year's, Thanksgiving, and Christmas days. There is a moderate admission fee. The mansion (717–665–7021) is north of Manheim on Route 72.

Mountains named for emotions seemed to abound in Dutch Country. When you're done at Mt. Hope, Route 772 takes you to Mt. Joy, a pleasant place to spend the night or have a meal at

Herskey Kiss Lamppost

◆**The Cameron Estate Inn.** Abe and Betty Groff, the innkeepers, are eighth-generation Lancaster County residents who've found a realistic way to keep an elegant inn in the countryside without going glitzy. The setting is so rural that if you walk to the end of the property, you step onto the farm of someone else. The inn is situated behind a church, surrounded by fields. You can't see it from the road. (When you make a reservation, the Groffs send you a map for finding the place.) The food tends to reflect today's lighter tastes, with an a la carte menu. Popular entrees include fresh fish, a chicken and shrimp dish, seafood cassoulet, smoked pork chops, and steaks. The inn has the requisite parlor fireplace and veranda, once the scene of heavy political discussion, as well as antique four-poster beds and Oriental carpets. Most of the eighteen rooms have private baths and some have fireplaces. Because of its historic designation, the Groffs can't build a swimming pool on the property, but guests are invited to use the pool at the Groffs' own home. Also, tennis is available nearby. The inn is open year-round, except for Christmas Eve and Christmas Day. Call (717) 653–1773.

Backtrack a couple of miles on Route 772 to Route 72 to head north, crossing the turnpike, to stop at Cornwall and inspect the ◆ **Cornwall Iron Furnace,** which produced cannon for the Revolutionary War. Before the war it produced stoves and farm tools, a classic case of guns or butter. Pennsylvania's iron deposits were the result of the hot water under the earth's surface dissolving the limestone in the rock and leaving the iron oxide as concentrated iron ore. The location of the furnace, in an area rich in iron deposits, limestone, and timber, made Cornwall a highly productive site. The furnace operated from 1742 to 1883, with workers stoking the fire and pouring molten iron around the clock. The mine was worked until 1972. The restored site includes the original furnace stack, blast machinery, open pit mine, ironmaster's mansion, and wagon and smith shops. The charcoal house is a visitor center displaying exhibits about all phases of mining. Hours are Tuesday through Saturday 9:00 A.M. to 5:00 P.M. and Sunday noon to 5:00 P.M. It's closed Christmas, Thanksgiving, and New Year's days. A modest admission fee is charged. Call (610) 589–2934.

THE BOLOGNA CAPITAL

It's a drive of only a few minutes from Cornwall up Route 72, back to Route 422 and Lebanon, home of Lebanon bologna. In the 1800s Pennsylvania German settlers made this sausage, each family concocting its own recipes and mixing in unusual seasonings. Today most of the Lebanon bologna eaten in the United States comes from the Lebanon Valley. No other bologna tastes remotely like it, nor does it taste quite the same if you eat it in some other state, no matter where it was made. The recipes are still secret, but the four manufacturers, at two locations, invite visitors, offer tours, maintain museum displays, and offer you good prices in salesrooms. From Route 422 the easiest stop is ◆ **Weaver's Famous Lebanon Bologna,** just off the highway, 1 mile east of Lebanon at Fifteenth Avenue and Weavertown Road. Signs direct you clearly. As you pull into the parking lot at Weaver's, you'll see stacks of firewood, notice the aroma of hardwood smoke, and then you'll watch workers hanging bolognas by hand in wood smokehouses, just as they would have done in the 1700s. The faint odor of smoked meats follows you throughout the plant. By the time you leave, you're ready to sink your teeth into a huge bologna sandwich. While you're there, if customers come in asking for "drops," they're asking for seconds, imperfect products that the company sells at a discount. Drops are nutritionally fine and perfectly safe, they just don't live up to the Weaver standards for one reason or another. A common problem is that the bologna is softer in the middle than around the edges, which makes it hard to slice. If you're trying Lebanon bologna for the first time, don't mess with drops; pay the full price and learn how it is at its best. The product doesn't have to be refrigerated as long as the package is sealed, so it's okay to carry it in the car. While you're buying bologna you can pick up a T-shirt with WEAVER'S FAMOUS LEBANON BOLOGNA emblazoned across the front. In Pennsylvania buying and wearing such a T-shirt makes perfectly good sense. Hours are Monday through Saturday, 9:00 A.M. to 4:00 P.M. Call (717) 274–6100 or (800) WEAVERS.

THE CHOCOLATE CAPITAL

Breathe deep in Lemoyne and you're already in Hershey. You'll know even if you don't see a sign, because the entire town smells endlessly like a pot of boiling cocoa. Lest you miss that clue, all the street lights look like tall posts topped with giant Hershey Chocolate Kisses wrapped in silver foil. Even the paper tail with the word *Hershey* on it streams properly from the top of the kiss. It's hard to know how much time in Hershey is enough and how much is too much, especially when you consider that the visitor center of ◆ **Hershey's Chocolate World** alone attracts more than a million and a half visitors a year. No Pennsylvanian breathes who hasn't heard of Hershey, and few live who haven't visited here at least once in their lives. You may not want to devote days to the attractions, but you should know about the phenomenon. Hershey is clearly a company town, exactly in the manner of a coal town or textile town, albeit more prosperous.

It all started with the Hershey bar. Today Hershey Foods Corporation comprises many other food manufacturing divisions, including one for macaroni products, but chocolate gets all the noncorporate, that is, *tourist*, attention. **Hershey Park**

108

(717–534–3916), an eighty-seven-acre theme park, has nearly fifty rides, including one of the oldest operating carousels in the country, and a zoo. Hershey's Chocolate World, the visitor center, gives simulated tour rides showing how chocolate is made. (In earlier times visitors toured the actual plant to see the manufacturing process, sampling chocolate milk and pieces of chocolate candy at the end.) You can shop and eat in an indoor tropical garden. Hours vary seasonally. Call ahead to (717) 534–4900. **Hershey Gardens** gives guided and unguided tours of its three-season, twenty-three-acre botanical gardens. The gardens are open daily April through December (717–534–3492). **Hershey Parkview Golf** (717–534–3450), an eighteen-hole golf course, ranks among the top twenty-five public courses in the country, according to *Golf Digest*. **Hershey Museum of American Life,** next to the park entrance, exhibits Pennsylvania Dutch antiques, American Indian artifacts, and memorabilia of founder Milton S. Hershey. Hours are Memorial Day to Labor Day, daily 10:00 A.M. to 6:00 P.M. and until 5:00 P.M. the rest of the year. It is closed Christmas, Thanksgiving, and New Year's days. A moderate admission is charged. Call (717) 534–3439.

THE STATE CAPITAL

When you've used up Hershey, you'll have to decide whether to stop in Harrisburg, the state capital, follow Route 322 into South Central Pennsylvania, or go north along the Susquehanna River to the center of the state.

Unquestionably, Hershey gets more hype than Harrisburg, even though Harrisburg is older and about ten times bigger. It started as a trading post in 1710 and even today remains a relatively small city, with a population of fewer than 60,000 and a small-town feel. The State Capitol Building is on Capitol Hill. Guided tours are available for free Monday through Saturday 8:30 A.M. to 4:00 P.M. Tours leave every hour weekdays and every half hour Saturday and Sunday except from noon to 1:00 P.M. Call (717) 787–6810.

The ◆**State Museum of Pennsylvania,** William Penn Memorial Museum, and Archives Building, on Third Street between North and Forster, displays the original charter King Charles II granted to William Penn. Other exhibits cover military history, science, industry, and decorative and fine arts. The complex houses a planetarium. Hours are Tuesday through Saturday 9:00 A.M. to 5:00 P.M. and Sunday noon to 5:00 P.M. The museum is closed major holidays, and admission is free. Call (717) 787–4978.

The ◆**Museum of Scientific Discovery,** at Third and Walnut streets, offers another kind of diversion. This is an interactive museum, meaning that you don't just look at the exhibits—you do things with them. For instance, in the "Hidden Kingdom" exhibit, you study microbes under magnification to learn about immunology, especially AIDS. In the "Bring Your Own" exhibit, you put what you have brought to the museum under a microscope with a zoom lens to study the samples at magnification up to forty-eight times. The museum also has many changing exhibits, including its share of dinosaurs. Open Tuesday through Saturday 9:00 A.M. to 5:00 P.M. and Sunday noon to 5:00 P.M.; closed holidays. A moderate admission fee is charged. Call (717) 233–7969.

Assuming you don't want to spend much time in a city, even a small one, you can get a good sense of what the old Harrisburg society must have been like by driving along the river on Front Street to look at the old mansions. High taxes and maintenance costs have forced families out of most of them, relegating them to offices for various agencies; consequently, they're now exquisitely landscaped and maintained.

Once you're outside Harrisburg on the west side of the Susquehanna River, you're only about 15 miles away from a neighboring town that one local resident calls "just a spit on the map," ◆**Boiling Springs.** The community is so small that the historical society that has the most information about it has a Carlisle address (Cumberland County Historical Society, 21 North Pitt Street, P.O. Box 626, Carlisle 17013). But Boiling Springs has become one of those little pockets of rustication/sophistication that attract novel enterprises, interesting people, and, ultimately, good food and lodging. Also, the town has enough important history and historical buildings to be worth your spending a day and maybe a night here.

In the eighteenth century, Boiling Springs was an iron-manufacturing settlement. It became a vacation village for the well-to-do in the nineteenth century. The town was involved in both the Revolutionary War and the Civil War and was a part of the underground railroad.

Boiling Springs Lake, a seven-acre man-made lake, dates back to the 1740s, when it was dammed to produce power for a gristmill. The lake is fed by at least thirty natural springs in subterranean caves. The springs bubble to the surface, making it look as though the lake is boiling—hence the name—but the water is not hot. Ask the kids who tried to cook an egg in it. The lake is reputed to offer some of the best trout fishing in the area, and if you need supplies, there's a fishing shop right in town.

A fairly sumptuous place to stay is **Allenberry,** a resort lodge with dining and theater, and access to a golf course. The lodge is a new construction with fifty-five rooms and appealing outdoor gardens. Open April to mid-November. Call (717) 258–3211.

The Boiling Springs Civic Association publishes a brochure mapping out a walking tour of the historic district, which includes buildings dating as far back as 1795 as well as old ironworks, stables, and an old forge with a restored blast furnace.

Boiling Springs Tavern, at the corner of First and Front streets (717–258–3614 for reservations), built circa 1832, is still a popular tavern and restaurant where you can enjoy something besides the ubiquitous Pennsylvania Dutch–style food. The building is stone, with casual French country decor and two stone fireplaces, one built in 1832, the other in 1950.

The tavern is open for lunch and dinner Tuesday through Saturday; it offers a great wine list, aged western beef, fresh fish prepared with fresh herbs, vegetarian specialties, and, generally, an American menu. Geoff and Debi Keith, who run the tavern, grow their own herbs in season.

You might take a side trip south of Harrisburg to the town of **Mount Joy.** If you're headed for Lancaster (certainly not an off-the-path kind of place any more) Mount Joy is right on the way on Route 283. Here you'll find **Bube's Brewery.** It is the only nineteenth-century brewery that is intact in its original condition in the United States. Because all the equipment is very old, the brewery does not actively brew beer, but it is a fascinating place to visit, shop, and dine. Visitors are usually boggled by the underground passages and catacombs and pleased by the outdoor biergarten.

Alois Bube, a German immigrant, bought a small brewery in

1876 because of the growing fondness Americans displayed for German-style lager instead of English-style ales. He expanded the brewery over time and built a Victorian hotel onto it as a place to serve his beer and then give the people who drank it a place to stay. He died, young—just fifty-seven—and wealthy. Because he left his family well off, they were able to live here until the 1960s without doing a thing to the brewery. That's how this one has survived, a period piece, when so many other breweries were chewed up in mass production.

There's a lot to do if you visit the preserved and restored brewery today: fine dining in the catacombs and hotel, casual dining in the bottling works, shopping in the cooper's shed, viewing the original art in the brewery gallery, and, of course, touring the brewery itself.

The Catacombs Restaurant is several stories below street level in what used to be the brewery's stone-walled aging cellars. The menu includes gourmet treatments of seafood, beef, and poultry. The prices range from about $16 to $24. The restaurant has a wine and beer list and a cocktail lounge. It's open seven nights a week beginning at 5:30 P.M. weekdays and 5:00 P.M. weekends. Special Roman and medieval feasts are often held on Sunday nights. Call (717) 653-2056 for more information.

The Alois restaurant is in the original bar and dining rooms of the old Victorian hotel. The menu here emphasizes variety from an international repertoire with recipes created by the chef, Oophelia Horn, to make the most of the tastes, textures, colors, and aromas of the individual ingredients. The food is served to background music, in a succession of courses that turns a meal into a theatrical experience. Reservations for the Alois restaurant are available Tuesday through Thursday from 5:30 to 9:00 P.M., Friday and Saturday from 5:00 to 10:00 P.M., and Sunday from 5:00 to 9:00 P.M. Call (717) 653-2057.

Eating in the Bottling Works is a more casual affair. This is a tavern and restaurant in the plant where beer and soft drinks used to be bottled and the water for making the beer was drawn from limestone caverns. Next door is an outdoor biergarten of the sort that Alois Bube probably went to in Bavaria. The boiler and smokestack that created steam power for the brewery stand in the middle of the garten. The menu includes steaks, seafoods, sandwiches, and salads. Live entertainment is presented on weekends, including jazz on Sunday evenings. The Bottling Works also features many special musical events by regional artists. They'll send you a schedule if you call (717–653–2160). Lunch is served seven days a week beginning at 11:00 A.M. Monday through Saturday and at noon Sunday. Dinner is served daily from 5:30 P.M. weeknights and 5:00 P.M. weekends. The bar opens daily at 11:00 A.M. except Sunday, when it opens at noon.

If you prefer you can tour the brewery without eating at the restaurants. Free guided tours are offered from June 15 to the day before Labor Day, on the hour, 11:00 A.M. to 4:00 P.M. Monday through Saturday and noon to 4:00 P.M. Sunday. You can make reservations for tours other times as well.

Bube's Brewery is at 102 North Market Street in Mount Joy, 1 block off Main Street (Route 230). Internet website: http://lancaster.net/bubes/

While you are in the area, it might be fun to stop at **Donegal Mills Plantation,** proof that all plantations aren't in the south. This one has a 250-year-old mansion, a mill and miller's house, gardens, and a bake house. Tours are available Saturday and Sunday noon to 6:00 P.M. from the middle of March to the end of December and by appointment. Admission is $4.00 for adults, $2.00 for children ages 6 to 12. Call (717) 653–2168.

APPENDIX

PENNSYLVANIA WINERIES

Touring wineries in Pennsylvania is as varied an activity as would be rummaging through attics in every part of the state—you'll find things you like and things you don't, but you'll never be bored. Touring just the Pennsylvania wineries could give you a vacation of several days or several weeks. Pennsylvania's grape harvest begins in the middle of August in the southeastern part of the state and ends in the middle of November in the northwestern area by Lake Erie. Pennsylvania has become the twelfth largest producer of wine in the United States, with about fifty licensed wineries.

There are many signs that Pennsylvania's wine industry is maturing. You can buy Pennsylvania wines at the state-controlled liquor stores, and the Liquor Control Board and the Department of Agriculture are working together to promote Pennsylvania wines. Wine shops are opening in malls and shopping centers. The Pennsylvania commerce secretary has said that wine and grape products "pump millions of dollars into the state's economy" every year. Pennsylvania ranks fourth nationally in grape production (and it ain't all going into jelly!). And more and more wineries are producing wines of increasing sophistication. Typically, a new winery starts out with rather sweet offerings. The wines get dryer as the wine maker and the wine buyer learn more about wine.

The Pennsylvania Wine Association has become increasingly professional in its operation. It publishes a tabloid-sized periodical devoted entirely to articles, listings, and advertisements about Pennsylvania wineries. For more information or a subscription, contact Howard Miller, Pennsylvania Wine Association, 103 South Duke Street, Lancaster 17602. Phone (717) 291–1130; fax (717) 291–2042. Subscriptions are free. You can also pick up free

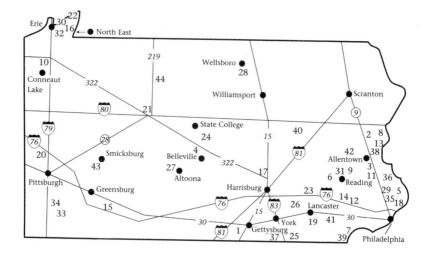

copies at member wineries. (Not all wineries in Pennsylvania belong to the association, though most do.) The following listings are from their publication, *Pennsylvania Wines and Wineries.*

1. Adams County Winery
251 Peach Tree Road
Ortanna, PA 17353
(717) 334–4631

Monday through Saturday, 12:30 to 5:00 P.M. Tastings and tours by appointment.

From Gettysburg, take Route 30 west for 5 miles, then bear left at the fork in the road. Follow old Route 30 to Cashtown, then go left onto Ortanna Road at the sign for Ortanna. Follow for 1 mile, go right at the T-intersection, and take an immediate left onto Scott School Road. Take a right onto Peach Tree Road and follow signs. An outlet store is located west of Gettysburg on Route 30 at the Pine Village Shops. The store is open Saturday and Sunday, 12:30 to 5:00 P.M.

2. Big Creek Vineyard
Route 1, Box 1101
Kunkletown, PA 18058
(610) 681–3959

Monday through Thursday 1:00 to 5:00 P.M., Friday and Saturday 1:00 to 7:00 P.M., Sunday 2:00 to 5:00 P.M. Follow Route 209 to Route 534 West and go ⅒ mile to Beltzville Road and then ⅗ mile to Keller Road. Turn left onto Keller Road and go ⅗ mile to the second driveway on the left.

3. **Blue Mountain Vineyards, Inc.**
   7627 Grape Vine Drive
   New Tripoli, PA 18066
   (610) 298–3068

Saturday and Sunday 10:00 A.M. to 6:00 P.M. and weekdays 4:00 to 7:00 P.M.

From Allentown, follow Route 309 north to route 143. Go left onto Route 143 for ¼ mile then right onto Madison for ½ mile. Take a right onto Grape Vine Drive; winery is on the left.

4. **Brookmere Farm Vineyards**
   RD 1, Box 53, Route 655
   Belleville, PA 17004
   (717) 935–5380

Monday through Saturday, 10:00 A.M. to 5:00 P.M. and Sunday 1:00 to 4:00 P.M. Tours and tasting.

Located on Route 655, 5 miles southwest of Route 322, in Belleville.

5. **Buckingham Valley Vineyards**
   1521 Route 413, P. O. Box 371
   Buckingham, PA 18912
   (215) 794–7188

Tuesday through Saturday, 11:00 A.M. to 6:00 P.M. and Sunday noon to 4:00 P.M.

Take Route 413 into Buckingham Valley. The winery is on Route 413, 2 miles south of Buckingham Village from Route 202.

6. **Calveresi Winery**
   107 Shartlesville Road
   Bernville, PA 19506
   (610) 488–7966

Thursday and Friday, 1:00 to 6:00 P.M., Saturday and Sunday noon to 5:00 P.M., other hours by appointment. Tours and tastings.

From Reading, go north on Route 183 for 10 miles. Take a right

117

at the Bernville Elementary School in Bernville and follow for ½ mile to winery on the right.

7. **Chaddsford Winery Limited**
   Route 1, Box 299
   Chadds Ford, PA 19317
   (610) 388–6221

Tuesday through Saturday 10:00 A.M. to 5:30 P.M. and Sunday noon to 5:00 P.M.

The winery is located on Route 1, 5 miles south of Route 202 intersection. From Philadelphia, take Route 95 south to Route 322 west. Take a left on Route 1 and continue for 6 miles. If traveling from Route 52 (Delaware), travel 1 mile north on Route 1 to winery.

8. **Cherry Valley Vineyards**
   RD 5, Box 5100
   Saylorsburg, PA 18353
   (717) 992–2255

Open daily 11:00 A.M. to 5:00 P.M.; free tours Saturday and Sunday only, 1:00 to 5:00 P.M.

Take Route 33 to the Saylorsburg exit to the winery.

9. **Clover Hill Vineyards and Winery at Breinigsville**
   9850 Newtown Road
   Breinigsville, PA 18031
   (610) 395–2468

Holiday hours: Monday through Saturday 10:00 A.M. to 5:30 P.M. and Sunday noon to 5:00 P.M. Tasting and gift shop.

Take Route 78/22 to Route 100 south. At the second traffic light, turn right onto Schantz Road and then left onto Newtown Road. Winery entrance is on the right.

10. **Conneaut Cellars Winery**
    Route 322, Box 5075
    Conneaut Lake, PA 16316
    (814) 382–6151

Open Monday through Saturday 10:00 A.M. to 6:00 P.M. Tasting, tours, and gift shop.

Take I–79 to exit 36B. Travel 6 miles on Route 322 west to Conneaut Lake. The winery is just before town on the left.

11. Country Creek Winery
133 Cressman Road
Telford, PA 18969
(215) 723–6516

Open Saturday noon to 5:00 P.M. Tasting and sales.
From Harleysville go 2½ miles west on Route 63. Turn right on Long Mill Road, left onto Moyer Road, cross the bridge, and turn right onto Cressman Road.

12. Fox Meadow Farm
1439 Clover Mill Road
RR 1, Box 312
Chester Springs, PA 19425
(610) 827–9731

Saturday and Sunday 1:00 to 5:00 P.M. Closed February and March. Tastings and tours.
Take Route 202 to Route 401 north. Travel 5 miles to Route 113 north. Continue 2^1/$_2$ miles and turn right onto Clover Mill Road. The winery entrance is ^{1}/$_4$ mile on left.

13. Franklin Hill Vineyards
Franklin Hill Road
RD 3
Bangor, PA 18013
(610) 588–8708

Monday through Saturday 11:00 A.M. to 4:00 P.M. Call for tours on Sundays.
From Route 22 East take Route 611 North to Pulcini's Restaurant. Make a left onto Front Street. At the top of the hill make a right onto Franklin Hill Road. Winery is on the right.

14. French Creek Ridge Vineyards
200 Grove Road
Elverson, PA 19520
(610) 286–7754

Open Saturday and Sunday noon to 5:00 P.M.
From the west take exit 22 off the Pennsylvania Turnpike onto Route 23 East. Go 6 miles then turn right onto Grove Road. From the east take exit 23 off the Pennsylvania Turnpike onto Route 100 North. Drive about 9 miles, take 23 West, go about 6 miles more, turn left onto Grove Road.

15. Glades Pike Winery
RD #6, Box 249D
Somerset, PA 15501
(814) 445–3753

June 1 to December 31 open daily noon to 6:00 P.M. January through May open Monday, Thursday, and Sunday noon to 6:00 P.M.

The winery is on Glades Road, now known as Route 31, 6 miles west of the Somerset exit (#10) and 13 miles east of the Donegal exit (#9) of the Pennsylvania Turnpike.

16. Heritage Wine Cellars
12162 East Main Road
North East, PA 16428
(814) 725–8015 or (800) 747–0083

Monday through Thursday 9:00 A.M. to 6:00 P.M., Friday and Saturday 9:00 A.M. to 8:00 P.M., Sunday noon to 6:00 P.M. Winter hours vary.

Take exit 12 off I–90. At U.S. Route 20; entrance across from McDonalds.

17. Hunters Valley Winery
Box 326D, RD 2
Liverpool, PA 17045
(717) 444–7211

Thursday 11:00 A.M. to 5:00 P.M., Saturday 11:00 A.M. to 5:00 P.M., and Sunday 1:00 to 5:00 P.M.

The winery is located on Routes 11 and 15, 2 miles south of Liverpool, 26 miles north of Harrisburg, and across the highway from the Millerburg Ferry.

18. In and Out Vineyards
258 Durham Road
Newtown, PA 18940
(215) 860–5899

Tasting and sales Staurday and Sunday 11:00 A.M. to 5:00 P.M., weekdays by appointment.

The vineyard is located on Route 413 about a half mile north of the Newton bypass and 3 miles south of Route 232.

19. Lancaster County Winery, Limited
799 Rawlinsville Road
Willow Street, PA 17584
(717) 464–3555

Monday through Saturday 10:00 A.M. to 4 :00 P.M. and Sunday 1:00 to 4:00 P.M.

Call for directions.

20. Lapic Winery, Limited
682 Tulip Drive
New Brighton, PA 15066
(412) 846–2031

Monday through Saturday 10:00 A.M. to 6:00 P.M. and Sunday 1:00 to 5:00 P.M.

Call for directions.

21. Laurel Mountain Vineyard
RD#1, Box 238
Falls Creek, PA 15840
(814) 371–7022

Open Wednesday through Sunday 10:00 A.M.. to 6:00 P.M. Closed in January.

From I–80 take exit 16. Go north 1⅘ miles on Highway 219 toward Brockway. Turn left at the first intersection onto Old Grade Road. Go 2 miles to the winery on the right.

22. Mazza Vineyards
11815 East Lake Road
North East, PA 16428
(814) 725–8695

Summer: Monday through Saturday 9:00 A.M. to 8:00 P.M.; Winter: Monday through Saturday 9:00 A.M. to 5:30 P.M.; Sunday, year-round, 11:00 A.M. to 4:30 P.M. Tasting and tours.

The vineyard is located 17 miles east of Erie and 6 miles from exit 11 of Route 90.

23. Mount Hope Estate and Winery
83 Mansion House Road
Manheim, PA 17545
(717) 665–7021

Open January through July, Monday through Saturday 10:00 A.M. to 5:00 P.M. and Sunday noon to 5:00 P.M.; July through December, Monday through Thursday and Sunday 10:00 A.M. to 6:00 P.M. and Friday and Saturday 10:00 A.M. to 7:00 P.M. Tastings, gift shop, tours, sales, and gift baskets.

Located 14 miles north of Lancaster on Route 72. Take exit 20 off the Pennsylvania Turnpike.

24. Mount Nittany Vineyard and Winery
RD 1, Box 138
Centre Hall, PA 16828
(814) 466–6373

Friday 1:30 to 5:00 P.M., Saturday 10:00 A.M. to 5:00 P.M., and Sunday 12:30 to 4:30 P.M.

The winery is located off Route 45, 3 miles east of Boalsburg. From Route 322, turn east on Route 45, pass the entrance to the Elks Country Club on your right, and take an immediate left onto Linden Hall Road. Proceed around the bend and down the hill, take a right at the pond onto Rock Hill Road, go through the Village of Linden Hall, take a left just before the church onto Brush Valley Road. Go right onto Houser Road toward the mountain, enter the woods, and continue on up the lane to the winery.

25. Naylor Wine Cellars, Inc.
RD 3, Box 424
Stewartstown, PA 17363
(717) 993–2431 or (800) 292–3370

Monday through Saturday 11:00 A.M. to 6:00 P.M. and Sunday noon to 5:00 P.M.

Tours, tastings, and gifts. Open year-round. Special groups by appointment.

Take exit 1 off Route I–83 to Route 851 east to Route 24. The winery is 2 miles north of Stewartstown.

26. Nissley Vineyards
140 Vintage Drive
Bainbridge, PA 17502
(717) 426–3514

Monday through Saturday 10:00 A.M. to 5:00 P.M. and Sunday 1:00 to 4:00 P.M.

Tastings, tours, and wine accessories.

From Lancaster take Route 30 West to Columbia. Exit at Route 441. Follow Route 441 for 8 miles. Turn right at Wickersham Road. Continue 1½ miles, following signs.

27. Oak Spring Winery
RD 1, Box 604
Altoona, PA 16601
(814) 946–3799

Open daily 11:00 A.M. to 6:00 P.M. Tours, tastings, and gift shop. Three miles north of Altoona Route 220, follow signs, Pine Croft exit off I–99/Route 220.

28. Oregon Hill Winery
RD 1
Morris, PA 16938
(717) 353–2711

Monday through Sunday 10:00 A.M. to 6:30 P.M. Tours and tastings.

Located off Route 287, 15 miles south of Wellsboro.

29. Peace Valley Winery
Box 94
Chalfont, PA 18914
(215) 249–9058

Open daily in December from 10:00 A.M. to 6:00 P.M., the rest of the year Wednesday through Saturday noon to 6:00 P.M. Tastings and gift shop.

From Doylestown, go northwest on Route 313 to New Galena Road. Turn left and continue for 2 miles to Old Limekiln Road. Turn right and proceed 1 mile to winery.

30. Penn Shore Vineyards
0225 East Lake Road
North East, PA 16428
(814) 725–8688

July and August, Monday through Saturday 9:00 A.M. to 8:00

P.M., September through June, Monday through Saturday 9:00 A.M. to 5:30 P.M., and Sunday 11:00 A.M. to 5:00 P.M. year-round.

Take exit 11 off I–90. Go north on Route 89 to Route 5. Proceed west on Route 5 for 2 miles. The vineyard is located 15 miles northeast of Erie on Route 5.

31. Pinnacle Ridge Winery
407 Old Route 22
Kutztown, PA 19530
(610) 756–4481

Open Saturday 10:00 a.m. to 5:00 p.m., Sunday noon to 5:00 p.m., and by appointment. Tastings and tours.

Take Route 22/78 to exit 12. (Kutztown, Krumsville, and Route 737). Go north on Route 737 to the blinking light in Krumsville. Turn right onto Old Route 22. The winery is located ⁹⁄₁₀ miles ahead on the left.

32. Presque Isle Wine Cellars
9440 Buffalo Road
North East, PA 16428
(814) 725–1314

Monday through Saturday 8:00 A.M. to 5:00 P.M. Closed Sundays. Tastings.

From I–90 West, take exit 12 (State Line Exit) to Route 20 West. Travel 6½ miles through North East town. Continue for 3½ miles past Route 89 to the winery entrance on the right, just past Catholic Cemetery Road.

From I–90 east, take exit 10 (Haborcreek Exit) to Route 531 North. Go north on Route 20 and turn right after 4 miles. The entrance will be on the left, 1 mile beyond Moorheadville Road.

33. Quaker Ridge Winery
211 South Wade Avenue
Washington, PA 15301
(412) 222–2914

Thursday and Friday 11:00 A.M. to 6:00 P.M. and Sunday noon to 5:00 P.M.

Located off U.S. 40 (National Pike) in downtown Washington. From the north, east, or west, take the Beau Street exit off I–70/79 and turn left toward Washington. At the first light turn left onto South Wade Avenue, and the winery is just past the next light.

From the south, take the Laboratory exit from I–79. Turn right and go through three traffic lights into town. Turn left onto South Wade Avenue and follow to winery.

34. Ripepi Winery and Vineyards
93 Van Voorhis Lane
Monongahela, PA 15063
(412) 258–3395

Monday through Saturday 11:00 A.M. to 6:00 P.M. and Sunday noon to 5:00 P.M. Tours available by appointment. Tasting and gift shop.

The winery is located off Route 88 near the junction of Routes 136 and 837.

35. Rushland Ridge Vineyard and Winery
2665 Rushland Road
P.O. Box 150
Rushland, PA 18956
(215) 598–0251

Saturday noon to 6:00 P.M. and Sunday noon to 4:00 P.M. Closed January through March.

From Route 263 take Almshouse Road east to fourth left. Take Rushland Road around second ninety-degree bend to winery.

36. Sand Castle Winery
Route 32, River Road, Box 177
Erwinna, PA 18920
(800) 722–9463

Monday through Saturday 10:00 A.M. 6:00 P.M. and Sunday 11:00 A.M. to 6:00 P.M.

The winery is located 2 miles south of the Frenchtown, New Jersey, bridge on Route 32 (River Road) just past the bridge over the Pennsylvania Canal. It is also 4½ miles north of Point Pleasant, Pennsylvania, on Route 32 just before the bridge over the Pennsylvania Canal.

37. Seven Valleys Vineyard and Winery, Limited
RD #4, Box 4660
Glen Rock, PA 17327
(717) 235–6281 (telephone and fax)

Tours and tastings by appointment.

From exit 1 on Route 83 at Shrewsbury, go west on Forest Avenue (Route 851) to the stop light at Main Street. Turn right and go ⁹⁄₁₀ mile to Clearview Drive. Turn left and go 1³⁄₁₀ miles to Gantz Road. Turn right and follow signs to the winery.

38. Slate Quarry Winery
460 Gower Road
Nazareth, PA 18064
(610) 759–0286

Friday, Saturday, Sunday 1:00 to 6:00 P.M. Tastings and tours.
Take Route 22 to 191 north to Nazareth. Veer left at blinker on Route 946 (past Newburg Inn). Cross over Route 248, $\frac{3}{4}$ mile to a group of houses, and veer right onto Knauss Road. There will be a sign $\frac{1}{2}$ mile down the road, bear right onto Gower Road. The winery entrance is $\frac{1}{4}$ mile on the right.

39. Smithbridge Winery
159 Beaver Valley Road
Chadds Ford, PA 19317
(610) 588–4703

Wednesday through Sunday noon to 5:00 P.M.
From the intersection of Route 202 and Route 1, go south on Route 202 for 1½ miles. Turn right onto Beaver Valley Road. Travel ½ mile and turn right into a gravel lane.

40. Susquehanna Valley Winery
802 Mount Zion Drive
Danville, PA 17821
(717) 275–2364

Wednesday through Sunday 1:00 to 6:00 P.M.
From I–80 east take exit 34 at Buckhorn. Follow Route 11 south toward Daneville. Just past the Jack Metzer Volkswagen/Jeep car dealership look for the winery sign on the right. Turn left on Ridge Drive and continue for 1 mile. At next crossroad, turn right onto Mt. Zion Drive and follow the signs into the winery.
Coming from I–80 west, take exit 33 at Daneville. Take Route 54 into Daneville until Route 11 turns left toward Bloomsburg. The winery sign is opposite the Jack Metzer Volkswagen/Jeep car dealership. Turn right on Ridge Drive and then right onto Mt. Zion Drive. Follow the signs to the winery.

41. Twin Brook Winery
5697 Strasburg Road, RD 2, Box 2376
Gap, PA 17527
(717) 442–4915

January 1 through March 31, Tuesday through Sunday noon to 5:00 P.M.; April 1 through December 31, Monday through Saturday 10:00 A.M. to 6:00 P.M. and Sunday noon to 5:00 P.M.

The winery is located 3 miles off Route 30 on the Chester/Lancaster County Line.

From Lancaster, travel 18 miles east on Route 30. Take a right onto Swan Road and follow the signs.

From Philadelphia and points east, take Schuylkill Expressway to 202 south to Route 30 west. Follow Route 30 west through Exton to the end of the Route 30 bypass. Continue west on Route 30 for 2⁷⁄₁₀ miles and take a left onto Swan Road. Follow the signs (3 miles) to the winery.

42. Vynecrest Winery, Inc.
172 Arrowhead Lane
Breinigsville, PA 18031
(610) 398–7525

Sunday through Thursday 1:00 to 6:00 P.M. Tasting and gift shop.

Take Route 78/77 to Route 100 south. At second traffic light on Route 100, turn right onto Schantz Road. Continue for 1⁸⁄₁₀ miles to Arrowhead Lane. Turn right and the winery entrance is on the left.

43. Windgate Vineyards
Box 213, RD 1
Smicksburg, PA 16256
(814) 257–8797

Open year-round noon to 5:00 P.M. except holidays. Tasting, tours, and gift shop.

From Pittsburgh, take Route 28 Expressway north to Kittanning and to Route 85. Turn right and follow Route 85 for 12 miles and then go left onto Route 839. At the SMICKSBURG - 3 MILES sign turn right. In Smicksburg, turn left onto Route 954 north and go 3 miles to Hemlock Acres Road. Turn left and go 2 miles.

From the Pennsylvania Turnpike, take exit 5. Follow Route 28 Expressway north to Kittanning. Follow the directions above.

44. The Winery at Wilcox
Box 39, Mefferts Run Road
Wilcox, PA 15870
(814) 929–5598

Open daily noon to 6:00 P.M. during the fall. Hours may vary the rest of the year.

Take Route 219 North of Johnsonburg. Turn right onto Mefferts Run Road. Drive 1‰ miles. The winery is on the left.

INDEX

UNITED STATES TRAVEL
Off the Beaten Path™ Series

These are the fine guides from our
Off the Beaten Path™ series designed for the traveler who enjoys
the special and unusual. Each book is by an author who knows the
state well, did extensive research, and personally visited many of
the places, often more than once.
Please check your local bookstore for fine Globe Pequot Press
titles, which include:

ALL TITLES $10.95 unless otherwise noted above.

To order any of these titles with MASTERCARD or VISA, call toll-
free (800) 243–0495; in Connecticut call (800) 962–0973. Free shipping for orders of three or more books. Shipping charge of $3.00 per
book for one or two books ordered. Connecticut residents add sales
tax. Ask for your free catalogue of Globe Pequot's quality books on
recreation, travel, nature, gardening, cooking, crafts, and more.
Prices and availability subject to change.